the
modern
bohemian
table

the modern bohemian table

Gathering with Friends and
Entertaining in Style

amanda grosgebauer bernardi

Published by Paige Tate & Co.
Paige Tate & Co. is an imprint of Blue Star Press
PO Box 8835, Bend, OR 97708
contact@paigetate.com
www.paigetate.com

ISBN: 9781944515942

Photography and writing by Amanda Bernardi

Book design and layout by Amy Sly

Illustration on page 19 by Alli Koch

Printed in China

10 9 8 7 6 5 4 3 2 1

for my mom, karen,

who taught me that details matter and tiny moments are the most magical.

and my son, alfeo,

who gave me a reason to slow down and enjoy every minute.

contents

introduction

We live in an age of plenty of goods and limited time. It is easier than ever to just buy-the-thing and do-the-thing. But when we look to the past too often, or merely imitate what we see in the present, we forget to look into ourselves, at our own experiences and tastes. As the world increasingly becomes more hectic, we constantly seek to create balance, well-being, and authenticity in our daily lives. Bohemianism has resurfaced in this search for a slowdown.

A bohemian is generally defined as someone who lives outside the status quo in their thinking and lifestyle. In the sixties and seventies, this looked like a clear rule-breaker, when living outside the norm was in defiance of structure and a threat to the old ways of doing things.

A modern bohemian is different. We have jobs and shave our legs, use technology regularly, and can generally walk down the street without attracting stares. Today's bohemians revolt not against the societal structure, but rather the slave to convention, the uniformity of the big-box store, and the mass taste influenced by social media.

A modern bohemian is focused on making their own way, true to self and creativity—less thinking, more feeling. Their style, in both their surroundings and their mindset, is inspired and tolerant—truth is valued more than perfection. Bohemian style is playful, affordable, and driven by the desire to stamp individualism on the world. It is about creating magic from the everyday and intention in every detail. Bohemian style extends creativity and permission to everyone to be themselves.

Entertaining and creating shared genuine moments with our favorite people is one small way we can break free from screen time and DoorDash and truly regenerate. There is nothing more nourishing than food for ourselves and our souls. It fosters community, hospitality, friendship, and love. Cavemen offered food as a peace offering to new friends. Then, with the invention of fire, they could socialize and celebrate a large kill and meal together. They could hunt and then gather.

Bohemian style has no rules, and neither does the bohemian way of entertaining. It is about creating truth and comfort. Filling bellies with laughter and flavor. It may not be formal, but it holds reverence for past traditions and pieces. This book will show you how you can bring the modern bohemian way of entertaining to your table, so you can create genuine and memorable moments with your favorite people.

First, we'll walk through the rules, traditions, and customs of table setting and entertaining, and then we'll learn how to break those rules, using the bohemian principles of design. We'll explore how to build a tabletop collection that can service all of your events, which you can build over time and on any budget. We'll chat about pre-party prep, how to stock the bar, and how to choose your wines. Then we'll put the collection to work in more than fifteen different party ideas, each of which includes a tablescape plan, menu, food and drink recipes, tips for the night, and DIYs and other tricks to personalize your gathering.

When I started my business, hunt & gather, I wanted to find those special pieces that could be shared and cherished by many people across many memorable moments. I spend time curating one-of-a-kind finds that authentically share the stories of my clients, while cutting back on event waste and cookie-cutter designs. As an event designer servicing nearly 100 events a year, I've helped my clients discover what it means for the event to truly represent themselves. This book is about granting you that same permission to throw the kind of party you want—and feel confident, comfortable, and true about every part of it!

what makes something bohemian?

Being bohemian does not mean throwing out all the rules to live a carefree, hairy-legged life (though it can mean that, if you like). More often, it means that you simply bend and embellish the standard design rules with your own preferences, experiences, and conveniences more than your un-bohemian neighbor might.

The general principles of design are taught to most interior designers or artists in their first class. It is what comes naturally to all of those people known to "have the eye." These days, we likely recognize these principles and picture them through our favorite social media accounts. Bohemian design and living still hold true to these rules but incorporate the following characteristics.

LAYERS & THE GIFT OF THE MIX-AND-MATCH

When it comes to creating interest and rhythm in a space or on a table, bohemians use all of the tools in the toolbox: color, shapes, texture—often all together, to create a layered experience. Picture stacked rugs on the floor, a painted wall mural behind hung photos, and big bold-colored furniture in a stark, white-walled room. Combinations as unique as each person, but all bold.

SUSTAINABLY MADE

Bohemians honor sustainability in their goods, which means they are either recycled, coined "vintage," or recently hand-made by someone paid a fair wage. Our belongings speak to our values. Concerns about waste, pollution, and treatment of workers are important to the story we tell through our purchases. We want goods that can withstand normal day-to-day living, and if it has survived thirty-plus years in someone else's home, it will likely withstand another thirty years. Not to quote every grandparent in the world, but: they just don't make things the way they used to. Plus, when you find a vintage, thrifted, or antique piece, it is likely unique and one of a kind, which makes it even more special.

INTERESTING CONTRASTS

With the mix of materials, colors, patterns, textures, and eras, the vibe stays interesting and nostalgic, yet modern. Just like our lives. Bohemians design their homes, events, and wardrobe to match their actual lives—and our lives are complicated, compelling, and contrasting. Bohemian style can be very relaxed and casual on one end, yet highly thought-out and detailed on the other. It is the perfect blend of life and design.

General Principles of Design

1. **REPETITION:** Repeating elements like color, shape, and textures unify spaces by creating a rhythm in the design with a consistent visual and physical experience.

2. **BALANCE:** Equality and symmetry in all elements. Balance can be symmetrical (more formal), asymmetrical (more relaxed), or radial (more focused on one moment).

3. **HARMONY:** The space and all of its parts relate to and complement each other. All elements act together to create a unified message.

4. **PROPORTION AND SCALE:** Proportion has to do with the ratio of one design element to another, or one element to the whole. Scale concerns itself with the size of one object compared to another.

5. **EMPHASIS:** A point of interest that can anchor the design and prevent the distraction of too much, or the boredom of no intentional interest.

ORGANIC BEAUTY

Bohemians tie in natural, living things as often as possible. With potted plants, dried florals, rocks, crystals, and more, you can share that organic beauty and energy in any situation. Plant lady is the new cat lady.

COLLECTED TREASURES

Bohemians are often collectors—we want to be surrounded by pieces that are filled with memories or inspiration—and typically not just one small collection, but several. This tendency mimics the feeling of overflowing with life. These material goods are the physical, authentic expression of all that bohemians hold dear. For me, my largest collection is books (not counting all of my "work" collections, which really just allow me a whole other excuse to collect things). Books stand in for memories, hopes, dreams, and all of the good I want to see and contribute to in the world. Most bohemian collections are of small, affordable things, as such items are both easier to hoard and easier to part with if you change your mind.

ORIGINAL

Bohemian design is original in that it usually entails unique, one-of-a-kind finds, due to the value of recycled and handmade goods. But bohemians also get creative in how they use their goods. Items might not always be used in the traditional way in which most people use them, but instead may be given a new, creative function. Imagine a birdcage as a plant stand, or an old door as a tabletop. Bohemians think outside the box for layout, function, and experience. The feeling of individuality and authenticity supersedes any prior notions of do's and don'ts. Bohemians are original because of the unique goods and uses for their treasures.

LIVED-IN

Bohemianism is not about perfection—it is about reality. So bohemian design is just that too. It is a bit messy and imperfect because it is used and enjoyed. Much to my mother's dismay, I don't own any furniture polish. I just switch out furniture for pieces that don't need upkeep, can withstand a lot of cozy nights, and can be layered with accessories to hide their imperfections. Bohemians are well-lived, and so are their goods and surroundings. You don't ever need to edit your life or your loves for the "supposed-to's."

how to set the table, build your collection, and throw a party

a brief history of entertaining

Food is something we all have in common. When we can savor the moment, as well as the meal, we are brought closer together. For the hunter-gatherers of the past, the whole production of the meal was a group effort. First in the hunt, then at the feast. Success in the hunt meant dinner for all. As humankind learned to grow plants and domesticate animals, we created a more complex variety of food, economy, and social network through sharing and exchange. Food became an instrument of status. Feasts became a sign of power, but also of social identity, as people came together as families, tribes, and communities.

Stories of shared dining were documented by the Ancient Greeks in the writings of Homer, and scenes of table settings are found in both the Old and New Testaments of the Bible. In the Middle Ages, there was little ceremony or custom when it came to food. Dining tables were simple boards placed over trestles, the actual practice of "setting the table." The boards were draped in fabric meant to be the shared napkin for the table. Knives were the first instrument used, then later spoons and cups were introduced and shared between guests. Food was stabbed with the knife, then placed on a small plank or large slice of bread.

The Renaissance brought on a search for enlightenment and personal care, which included ridding the habit of eating with one's fingers. A new canon of dining rules and utensils was introduced: plates, specific glassware, napkins, fine linens, and individual cutlery. Dining etiquette became a clear way to delineate between class lines, as wealth allowed for a larger collection and quality of tableware. The finest of dining became an event defined with silver utensils flanking plates of beautiful porcelain and delicate crystal stemware. Etiquette was a status symbol, whereby one could be tested by knowing how to use all pieces properly. As the middle class began to adopt the code, old manners lost their prestige and began to become more and more refined and specific to distinguish the proper folk from the common folk. But as customs continued to pass through all social ranks, more and more rules, refinement, and specificity piled on until both the upper and middle classes had evolved elaborate sets of rules for dining.

Today, as our modern lives became more focused on work, we see a lot of these rules come out only for special occasions, as ordinary meals are shorter and customs pushed aside for convenience. In our search for a slowdown and a retreat from our technology-driven, fast-paced day, turning back to the tradition of shared feasts is the perfect solution to preserving our cultural and individual sanity.

setting the table

Most people are familiar with their basic dinnerware and utensils and where items should be placed for a meal. By knowing the historical rules, you can create a table where everyone feels comfortable and not distracted by wondering which pieces to use and how to eat. A bohemian table can please grandmothers and kids alike—you'll pay tribute to the tradition but leave the stuffy rules behind.

A place setting is like a puzzle. Each piece has a place and is there for a reason so you can complete the meal. When you set the table according to the order by which you will eat, guests can simply move down the line. If the piece will not be used, then it shouldn't be on the table. No soup; no soup spoon. That's all there is to it. In both formal and casual dinner place settings, utensils, plates, and glassware are arranged in the order of use and clearing. While the rules may seem more complex, if you stick to this simple rule of placement, your guests will easily feel comfortable dining.

WHERE TO SET THE PIECES

- Place the dinner plate in the center of the table setting (charger underneath, if using). If you're serving salad, set the salad plate on top of the dinner plate.

- Place the fork to the left of the plate. If you're serving salad, set the salad fork to the left of the dinner fork.

- Place the knife to the right of the dinner plate with the blade facing in, and then set the dinner spoon to the right of the knife.

- Set the water glass in the top right corner, above the knife.

- Place the wine glass (red or white, depending on what you're serving) to the right of the water glass. If you're offering both types of wine, place the white next to the water and the red behind it.

- Place the bread plate above and to the left of the dinner and salad plates to balance out the glassware. The butter knife can be placed horizontally on the bread plate.

- Place the dessert spoon horizontally above the dinner plate.

- Add a place card above the dessert spoon. If the card is placed upright, write the guest's name on both sides. That way the guest can find their seat, and the guests on the other side of the table will know who they are talking to.

- Place the napkin on top of the dinner plate or beneath the fork, based on your preference.

Casual place setting: salad fork, dinner fork, salad plate, dinner plate, napkin, knife, wine glass, water glass

Formal place setting: salad fork, dinner fork, bread plate, butter knife, salad plate, dinner plate, napkin, knife, dinner spoon, dessert spoon, red wine glass, water glass

SERVING THE FOOD

But why is the fork on the left side when most people use it with the right hand? In medieval times, the knife was the predominate utensil, with the fork introduced to simply hold the meat while cutting with your stronger hand. European etiquette evolved to maintain that tradition. Today, you will see Europeans cut with their right hand while holding the fork in their left hand, tines down, then flip the tines up to serve the bite. Americans choose to keep the custom of the fork-on-the-left place setting, but switch the fork to their dominant hand unless they need to use the knife—the eat-and-switch method.

There are many different ways to serve dinner, and the serving style can have as big of an impact as the place setting in creating comfort and conversation. There are three main serving styles:

- **FORMAL:** This style is what you experience at a formal wedding, wherein waiters offer food to each guest, so no serving dishes appear on the table. The table is set and food is brought to each individual sequentially through the courses, with the table being cleared between each plate. Pretty fancy, but this style could be used for a super-special occasion in your home where you hire out experienced catering staff.

- **FAMILY STYLE:** This style has been the new rage at bohemian weddings and events. The serving dishes of food are placed on the table or on a table close by, and then passed around until everyone has served themselves. Typically, dessert is served later, while all other courses are served at the same time.

- **BUFFET:** In this style, all of the serving dishes are set up in a separate service area with a stack of plates. Each guest goes down the line filling up their own plate and no serving dishes come onto the table.

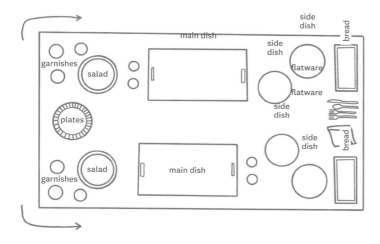

Buffet table set up conveniently for service

Family style is a great practice for a dinner party of eight to ten guests, where the table and conversations are more cozy and intimate. Buffet service is great for a larger party or guests of various ages (because you don't want the little ones pouring chimichurri down themselves). When setting up the buffet table, think about flow and logistics. You want the service area to be accessible before, during, and after the meal for refills for your guests and refills of each dish from the kitchen. Foods intended to complement each other should be grouped near each other— for example, salad dressings near the salad. Desserts can be added at the end of the table or rolled out later to the buffet table—or literally rolled out on your bar cart.

With a clear understanding of the "supposed-to's" you can start to bring in the personality and character that makes the table feel like the environment you want to create. But first, let's talk about how to pull together a collection of pieces that can carry you through different themes, seasons, designs, and formalities.

building an entertaining and servingware collection

Entertaining and sharing a meal with your people should not be about spending a ton of money or time following the rules. You want to create memorable moments without an inspiration mood board, twenty errands, and running up your credit card bill. With a thoughtfully curated collection of pieces, built over time through hunting, gifting, and inheritance, you can be prepared for unique gatherings every time.

DAILY COLLECTION

- Dinner plate
- Salad plate
- Flatware
- Water glass or goblet

You'll want enough dinnerware for your core people to be able to sit down to dinner with you for a formal-ish meal—not every extended family member or acquaintance, but who you expect to share special meals or holidays with you. Twelve to sixteen is usually a safe bet for the main dining items.

For all of these pieces, I suggest buying from a time-honored retailer who specializes in dinnerware. Gone are the days of matching and intricate patterns. Go with a classic, solid white. White dinner plates are not only versatile, but put the spotlight on the food. Salad plates are a great piece for which to have multiple designs, due to budget and size. Have your classic white set, but also pair with other designs that can brighten your everyday dinners.

Glassware, too, can be flexible. The only rule for glassware is that it holds liquid and can you sip from it without dripping. You can always mix and match colors and shapes. A good start is a clear, matching set and a mix-and-match color set in your favorite colors. You are also allowed to have more than one set of dinner plates! Plan for what best fits your storage and lifestyle. If you only have room for one set, go versatile with white, but you can certainly build out other sets, whether matching or assorted as your space allows.

I call this the daily collection because you should feel free to actually use the dinnerware you have. Using your dinnerware shouldn't cause you anxiety or guilt. Even if your grandmother kept the plates locked away, only to use once a year, it doesn't mean you have to. Joy weighs more than "supposed-tos." She would want you to enjoy her gift to you—maybe not every night on a folding tray in front of the television, but often enough throughout the year to warrant the storage space. If you worry about your guests, don't. When they see you've put time into creating a beautiful space, they'll respect it and be on their best behavior without being put on notice. Using your inherited pieces is a great way to pay tribute to your family memories and tradition as often as possible.

DAILY ADDITIONS

- Soup bowls
- Pasta bowls
- Fruit bowls
- Mugs
- Cups and saucers

Bowls are likely one of the most used pieces in your everyday life but are rare for a formal dinner setting. Because of this, having sixteen matching soup bowls, sixteen matching pasta bowls, and sixteen matching fruit bowls is not necessary. If used for a gathering, bowls can stand out as a colorful accent, or they can be mixed and matched. Buy the bowls that work best for what you enjoy in your day-to-day life. If you often make soup or chili for friends, mix and match your fruit bowls with your cereal bowls, and even with your favorite coffee mugs, and surprise people a bit with new ways to look at their favorite pieces.

ENTERTAINING COLLECTION

- 2 large platters
- 4 medium platters
- 2 large bowls
- Soup tureen
- Gravy boat
- 3 to 5 cake stands or pedestal plates

- 3 to 4 sets of serving utensils
- Unlimited wood boards
- Unlimited condiment or small serving bowls
- Unlimited baskets

The only rule for your entertaining collection is this: every piece should be special to you or tell a story you want to share. Have fun exploring thrift stores and antique stalls to choose each piece individually. If you love it, it will go well with everything else—no need to worry too much about a full matching collection. Everything on which you share precious budget or storage space should inspire joy.

ENTERTAINING ADDITIONS

- Appetizer, bread and butter, or dessert plates
- Steak knives

While these items are not all required, this mix is a great base with which to be able to serve a large formal meal like Thanksgiving dinner. For some gatherings, you may use only boards or baskets, but you can keep these pieces tucked around the house to use regularly in other roles, rather than feeling like you need to store a full range for a few meals a year.

Dessert and salad plates can be used interchangeably, allowing for a lot more options in your collection. Appetizer, bread and butter, or canapé plates are generally smaller than dessert and salad plates and can be used before dinner or as accents on a dinner plate. Nothing makes guests feel fancier than special cocktail plates or napkins.

There is nothing worse than watching guests gnaw away at a piece of beautifully prepared meat. Steak knife sets can often be found on sale racks at big-box stores or preserved at estate sales or antique malls—great for wedding registries and Christmas gift lists alike. Foodies can geek out over a good steak knife. It is a small piece that makes a huge difference in the enjoyment of the meal.

GLASSWARE

- 1 large pitcher
- 1 drink dispenser
- 2 carafes

Save yourself trips to and from the kitchen by readily having refills available for all with a pitcher on or near the table.

LINENS

- 3 to 4 dinner napkin options (sets of up to 20)
- 2 cocktail napkin options (sets of up to 20)
- Tablecloths or table runners

This is the easiest category to build a collection of multiple designs and sets, due to pricing, availability, and storage space.

When considering linens, forget the idea of pressed and perfect monogrammed art pieces. Fabric is a more sustainable option, but only when you plan on using them again. Having a few mix-and-match solid colors or patterns will allow for endless possibilities. While for a formal dinner you would want a 12-inch hang off of the table for a tablecloth, you don't always have to use traditional pieces that are the exact size of the table for other types of dinner parties. You can use linens from around the house—blankets, wall tapestries, sheets, etc.—to bring in more variety without spending any money. Raw fabric, whether vintage or new, can easily be morphed into table linens, often without much sewing. All of my napkins are vintage or made by my family. I'll order a few yards of fabric, rip the squares to size and do a quick hem as needed. Some fabrics need no sewing at all and can be ready to go in minutes. (See the resource guide for more info on DIY fabric options, page 216.)

A NOTE ON TABLECLOTHS: Many of my events do not incorporate a tablecloth. This is because I believe your table, just like everything in your life, is meant to be enjoyed and used. Unless you are covering your table to make for easy cleanup, don't be afraid to let the table be bare. If it gets a scratch or a ring, it's a memory of a good time with friends and family.

My advice to my wedding clients is that if they are going to order cocktail napkins for their wedding, get a design or saying that matters, not their wedding date. This way they can pull them out for gatherings after the wedding and they will seem intentional—not just like wedding leftovers.

BAR COLLECTION

- 8 to 12 wine glasses (match your dinner plate quantity)
- 4 to 8 double old-fashioned glasses
- 4 to 8 highball glasses
- 4 copper/brass mugs
- 2 shot glasses
- 1 shaker or mixing glass (with strainer)
- Bartender spoon
- 1 bottle opener/corkscrew
- 1 measuring shot glass or jigger
- 1 mixing spoon
- Beverage/ice bucket

Drinking or serving alcohol is not required to be a bohemian! If yours is a dry or sober home, some of these pieces are still fun to have for specialty cocktails (or mocktails) for guests, or just to add a bit of flair to your tabletop.

Just like your servingware collection, you will know the perfect combination for you. If you do not like liquor, then perhaps you'll have various types of beer steins or pilsner glasses. Regional and cultural influences play a role here too. Coloradans love their mules, so copper mugs are a must. Texans need their margaritas, and Californians need all the wine glasses. This is also a time to play to your strengths and have glassware that matches your favorite recipes to share.

DECOR COLLECTION

- 10+ taper candle holders (Brass is a great choice because it pleases grandmothers and best friends alike—modern and classic.)

- 12+ votive holders (metallic or clear, or incorporate your favorite color family)

- 3 small boxes or pedestals (to place family-style food, elevated florals, or candles on)

- 3 to 5 lanterns or large pillar candle holders

- Vases (wide-mouthed for large arrangements, bud vases, or mix and match)

- Small houseplants (Whether cacti or blooms, small plants with pots up to 4 or 5 inches tall can be perfect on the table—and anywhere else—year-round.)

This is the category that will shift and change the most. When it comes to budget, a little can go a long way. You can DIY some paper crafts, find a small collection of figurines from a thrift store, or pick up a decorative tile sheet from your local hardware store. These can be pieces you keep and reuse, or gift to your guests. Any effort brings a special touch that guests will appreciate. Never feel as if your tables are not Pinterest-worthy. Guests are not coming for the Instagram photos. They are coming to share a special meal with you.

A DETAILED GUIDE TO THE PIECES

Type	Size/Details	Uses	Quantity
dinner plate	10 to 11 inches in diameter	to plate the main course of a meal	12 to 18, depending on size of family
salad plate	7.5 to 8.5 inches in diameter	to plate the salad or first course of a meal	12 to 18
soup bowl	9 to 10 inches in diameter	wide, shallow bowl with a rim for soups and liquids—the only bowl used in formal dinner service	6
pasta bowl	8 to 9 inches in diameter	a wide, tall rimmed bowl to hold pasta or other sauced grains	6
fruit / cereal bowl	5 to 8 inches in diameter	used with food eaten with a fork, mainly for informal meals	6+
coffee cup and saucer	holds 6 to 8 ounces	used for hot beverages, such as coffee, tea, cocoa, or cider; paired with a small plate to catch spillage	6
coffee mug	holds 11 to 12 ounces	used for the above hot beverages, but traditionally less formal	6+
espresso cup and saucer	holds 1 ounce (single) or 2 ounces (double)	used for strong or thick hot beverages, such as espresso or hot chocolate made from paste	6
charger plate	11 to 14 inches in diameter	serves as a placeholder for the dinner plate and can be left on the table as a base for all courses	match dinner plate quantity for formal setting
bread and butter plate	6 to 6½ inches in diameter	small dish used for rolls or bread	match dinner plate quantity for formal setting
dessert plate	6½ to 7½ inches in diameter	small dish used to serve dessert; can be used for other small-plate purposes	12+
serving platter	12 to 18 inches across	various shapes and sizes; can hold a side dish or main dish	6+
wooden serving platter	12 to 18 inches across	various shapes and sizes; can hold a side dish or main dish	mix and match with quantity above
serving bowl	9 to 16 inches across	nesting bowls are a smart space saver	mix and match with quantity above
soup tureen	holds 2 to 4 quarts; sized slightly larger than a football	used to serve soup and other liquid-based dishes	1
gravy boat	holds 5 plus ounces; a designated boat or sub in any small ceramic pitcher that can hold heat	used to serve gravy and other sauces	1 to 2
cake stand / pedestal platter	8 to 14 inches across; various heights	used to plate cakes and pies or to hold decorative pieces; pedestals also add height to a table or buffet	1+
condiment bowl	2 to 4 inches in diameter	used to hold condiments and sauces (pickles, olives, mustard, etc.)	unlimited
dinner fork	7 inches in length	used to eat the main course in all formal and informal meals	match dinner plate quantity, plus some
salad fork	6 inches in length	used in formal and informal dinning for salads and appetizers	match dinner plate quantity, plus some
dinner knife	9 inches in length	used for all courses and all types of meals	match dinner plate quantity, plus some
dinner spoon (tablespoon)	6½ to 7½ inches long	all-purpose spoon	match dinner plate quantity, plus some

Type	Size/Details	Uses	Quantity
coffee spoon (teaspoon)	5½ to 6½ inches in length	used mainly in informal dining to stir hot beverages	match dinner plate quantity, plus some
steak knife	8 to 9 inches long with a serrated edge	used with thick portions of meat	match dinner plate quantity for formal setting
serving utensils	12 to 16 inches long; made of several different types of materials	used to dish a full serving of main dishes or side dishes	6+
tumbler glass	holds 8 ounces	used for water, juice, or soda	match dinner plate quantity, plus some
goblet glass	holds 10 to 12 ounces	used for water, juice, or soda	match dinner plate quantity, plus some; can be used in place of tumblers
wine glass	holds 8 to 12 ounces	red wine glasses are larger to encourage oxidation; white wine glasses are narrower	match dinner plate quantity for formal setting
champagne glass	holds 6 to 10 ounces	tall narrow flute prevents the fizz from going flat	6+
highball glass	holds 8 to 9 ounces	used to serve tall cocktails and other mixed drinks	4+
old-fashioned glass	holds 6 to 8 ounces (single) or 12 to 14 ounces (double)	used to serve spirits and cocktails	4+
pilsner glass	holds 7 to 14 ounces	made to showcase paler ales but can be used for any beer	4+
cocktail / coupe glass	holds 5 to 7 ounces	used to serve iceless cocktails	4+
pitcher	holds up to 2 quarts	used to serve cold beverages	1+
carafe	holds 1 to 2 quarts	used to serve cold beverages or wine	1+
decanter	holds up to 25 ounces, or one bottle of wine	used to serve and oxidize wine or other alcoholic liquids	1+
shot glass	holds up to 1½ ounces	used for measuring alcohol for a cocktail, or as a shooter	1+
mint julep cup	holds 12 to 15 ounces	used to serve mint juleps and other assorted cool drinks in warm weather	as needed
Moscow mule mug	holds 14 to 16 ounces	used to serve Moscow mules or other cold beverages	as needed
drink dispenser	holds between 1½ to 3 gallons	used to hold and serve water or other cold beverages	1+
dinner napkin	20 to 24 inches	used at super-formal events	match dinner plate quantity for formal setting
lunch napkin	14 to 18 inches	the most commonly used size of napkin for all meals	as needed
cocktail napkin	4 to 6 inches	used with your drink to help with condition, temperature, and cocktail snacks—the fancy koozy	as needed

variations in your collection

True creativity comes in the challenge of arranging your collection into new and memorable combinations. Your everyday evenings and last-minute entertaining will be built with pieces in your collection. With a strong set, you can create a multitude of combinations with small accents or trimmings for endless possibilities for even the most casual of meals.

- White Dinner Plates
- White Salad Plates
- Wooden Dinner Plates

- Wooden Salad Plates
- Gold Flatware
- Wood and Metal Flatware

- Vintage Flatware
- Water Glasses
- Red Wine Glasses

- Assorted Glassware
- Assorted Napkins
- Assorted Table Linens

how to bring your bohemian vibe to your tabletop

Search Pinterest today for tablescapes and you'll find a multitude of interesting and artistic tables. But the biggest questions I want you to ask yourself when you're designing your tables are: What do I want people to feel? What do I want people to remember and cherish about this gathering?

To get started, I have some time-tested questions that can reveal all you need to consider when setting your table, no matter the event.

START WITH THE FOOD: WHAT WILL WE EAT IT ON?

The plate and the table are actually the most flexible pieces in a creative design. Whether it's a coffee table, kitchen island, or dining room table, look for a flat surface to gather around. In addition to a dining table that seats eight, I keep regular props on hand to create other spaces: biergarten folding tables; wide, flat side tables; old doors, boards, and sawhorses; and crates to lower the tables onto vintage rugs or quilts layered underneath. Dining room or driveway, you can easily recognize a table and know what to do with it.

The main purpose of the dinner plate is to hold the goods. When it is placed in the universally understood place for the dinner plate, it doesn't matter too much what shape it is, or what it is made from, so long as it complements the main activity: eating. Some dinners might be best served on a breadboard, a sheet of wax paper, or a small baking tray.

WHAT DO WE NEED TO EAT THE MEAL?

Staying true to the tradition of using only the pieces needed and placing them in the order of use, choose glassware, flatware, and napkins to complement the design. The only rule is to keep it to scale. When you combine dishes and flatware from different periods and styles, make sure that they share similar proportions, or scale.

HOW DO I GARNISH THE TABLE TO ENHANCE THE MEAL?

After adding the useful pieces, you can add in those that offer additional convenience and visual or conversational interest.

You have your basic utensils needed to eat the meal, but what will make dinner go over even easier? Can you add a water or wine carafe to the table so everyone can feel free to keep refilling their glasses? What about salt and pepper cellars so guests can season their food to their own tastes? This is also a time to get fancy with your "add-ons." For example, if you're serving bread, have a butter keeper but also some mashed garlic and a small olive oil bottle.

HOW DO I PERSONALIZE THE PLACE SETTINGS FOR THE NIGHT OR THE INDIVIDUAL GUESTS?

When I talk about personalization, I'm not just talking about name cards. While they appear in almost every image you pull up on Pinterest, place cards are not required nor appropriate for every meal or party you have. Sometimes deciding where people should sit can become an extra chore you don't have time for. I love a name card, but I typically choose some other accessory for the place setting instead. I want something that is personal both to me and to my guests. Whether a little trinket I've collected or a hand-drawn card, there are many ways to show care and attention to each place setting and guest without a personalized name card.

For place cards, I kind of cheat in that I still have all of the name cards from my wedding and can pull out family and friends from that little box when needed. My dad cut business card–sized rectangles from a large piece of acrylic, then my friend wrote everyone's name in modern calligraphy on each card. He cut a lot of blanks too, so I can quickly grab a paint pen and fill in a name as our family and community grow.

Personalization extends to all of the decor on the table. Taper candles are not required for every formal dinner party table. A centerpiece is not a must-have. Your table should reflect the overall energy and effort of the gathering, which is completely personal to you. I set my tables to be pretty, but not perfect. I leave old wax dripping down the sides of the candleholders, and lay greenery down the center of the table to cover up scratches. There is no perfect combination for decor, no standard punch list. I keep these basic rules in mind:

- Don't make things difficult. Either for you, as you prep the table, or for the guests sitting at it. If you love floral arranging, then bang it out. But don't sign up for something that you are not going to love creating. This is about moment-making for you and your guests. Don't add to your own frustration. For guests, keep it simple. They can easily tip a plate to move something, but if you build out a full Cézanne still-life scene on everyone's salad plate, they'll be left a bit confused when the bowl of salad is passed around: Do we bite into these pears or serve salad? Are the pears for the salad? When it comes to the

center of the table, make sure people can still converse across the table to one another. Keep any centerpieces low and modest.

- Waste not, store not. The more you have, the more you store or throw away. To keep your budget and waste level in check when building up your collection of decor items, plan for pieces that bring the most variety yet still show off your personality or the specific vibe of the gathering.

HOW DO I ENHANCE THE MOOD TO POUR OFF THE TABLE?

It is not all about the table, because at a good party, you're all over the place, not just sitting down for a quick shared meal. How will you interpret the mood across every moment of the party? How are guests greeted when they come in?

- **BAR/DRINK STATION:** Whether water or wine, guests will need a little something as soon as they arrive. Setting up a designated area for self-service will help you and your guests. Whether a designed bar cart, utility cart, side table, console table, or counter space in the kitchen, just create a space that is easy for guests to find and for you to refill as necessary. It is easy to get carried away with specialty drinks, but never forget a carafe or pitcher of water.

- **LIGHTING:** Generally, when you are inside, you have some overhead or pendant lighting to light up the room. If you need to tone down the overhead lights, bring in a table lamp or add more candles or lanterns on and around the table. Outdoors, think about string lights, hanging or floor lanterns, and candles on the table. Quiet and intimate = less lights. Bright and fun = more lights.

- **ENTERTAINMENT:** This boils down to music and games. For music, I generally like music that is fun for everyone (think early rock-n-roll or blues) or is nostalgic (e.g. early 2000s pop) to keep the mood light and inspire conversation. For games, I take the same approach: fun or nostalgic. Whether a new phone app or a vintage board game from the thrift store, be flexible with the mood of the gathering. Never hesitate to spontaneously play the piano or guitar for bonus memory points!

- **GATHERING AREAS:** Sometimes you might still be finishing up something in the kitchen and guests will inevitably gather around to help or just converse with you. To help spread the love, make sure you've consciously thought about where you would want people to hang, if not at the table. Can you distribute some snacks to the coffee table or patio? Add some candles so it seems inviting and intentional? The table is set, but what about all of the other gathering areas you want to create so guests don't crowd or stand around lost?

napkin folds

Uniquely folded napkins make a place setting shine—and they are a lot simpler to create than they seem! With just a bit of practice, you can create any unique napkin fold to customize and dress up your table.

FLATWARE POCKET

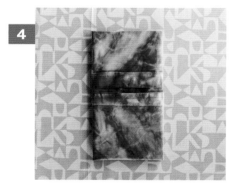

1 Lay the napkin out as a square with the finished side facing down.

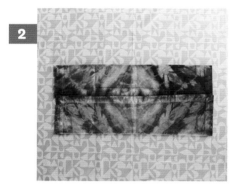

2 Fold the lower edge up about 3 inches, forming a horizontal band at the bottom of the napkin. Fold the upper edge down to meet the edge of the previous fold.

3 Flip the napkin over, keeping the same sides up and down. Fold the right edge in to the vertical centerline of the napkin. Fold the left edge in to the center.

4 Fold the left edge over to the right edge.

5 Arrange the napkin with the larger rectangle at the bottom. Slide flatware into the pocket for each place setting.

FORTUNE COOKIE

1. Lay the napkin out as a diamond with the finished side facing down. Fold the upper point down to the lower point, forming a triangle.

2. Holding the middle of the upper edge, fold the left point down to the lower point, then the right point down to the lower point, forming a diamond.

3. Picking up the napkin from the right and left corners, fold the lower half of the diamond under the upper half, forming a triangle.

4. Gently bring the lower right and left points closer together, raising the napkin to an upright position.

5. Position the napkin on an angle, adding a fortune or name card.

FLOWER BOUQUET

Lay the napkin out as a diamond, with the finished side facing up, then fold the upper corner down to the bottom corner, forming a triangle.

Holding the middle of the upper edge, fold the left point down to the lower point, then the right point down to the lower point, forming a diamond.

Fold the lower edges in to the vertical centerline, forming a kite shape.

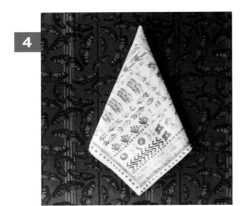

Flip the napkin over and fold the upper points down, leaving a pocket down the center.

Arrange on the plate, tucking in the bottom point if it's too large for your plate. Add flowers in the pocket.

DIAGONAL

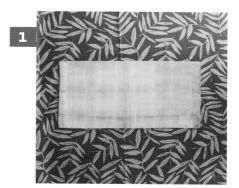

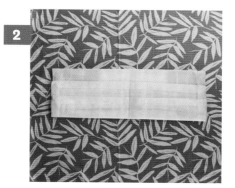

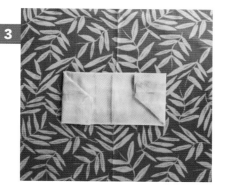

Lay the napkin out as a square, with the finished side facing down, then fold the lower edge up to the upper edge, forming a horizontal rectangle.

Fold the top layer of the upper edge back down, leaving a 2- to 3-inch band of fabric showing below the edge. Fold the railing layer of the top edge down over the newly folded edge, creating an upper band that is the same width as the lower one.

On each side, fold the lower left corner up to the horizontal centerline, forming a small triangle, then fold inward, meeting the edge of the triangle.

Fold the lower corners up to the center, forming a triangle on top of the napkin.

Flip the napkin over and arrange on the plate.

HEART

1

Lay the napkin out as a square, with the finished side facing down, then fold the lower edge up to the upper edge, forming a horizontal rectangle.

2

Fold the lower edge up to the upper edge again, forming a narrower rectangle.

3

Rotate the napkin so the fold is at the top and the loose ends are at the bottom. Holding the middle of the upper edge, fold the right half, then left half down to the vertical centerline.

4

Flip the napkin over, keeping the point up and the tails down. Fold the corners in on each side to meet at the vertical centerline of each tail, forming two points.

5

Flip the napkin over and arrange with the point facing down.

WINDMILL

1

Lay the napkin out as a square with the finished side facing down, then fold each corner into the center, forming a diamond.

2

Rotating the napkin as a square, fold the left edge over to the vertical centerline. Fold the right edge over the vertical centerline, forming a vertical rectangle.

3

Fold the lower edge up to the horizontal centerline and the upper edge down to the centerline, forming a square. Loosen the two tips from inside the top layer on each side of the square, pulling them out to form a point.

4

Fold the upper half of the left point so that it points straight up, perpendicular to its original position. Then fold the lower half of the right point so that it points straight down, perpendicular to its original position.

5

Center on the plate.

ENVELOPE

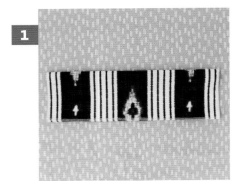

1

Lay the napkin out as a square, with the finished side facing down, then fold the napkin into three equal parts, forming a horizontal rectangle.

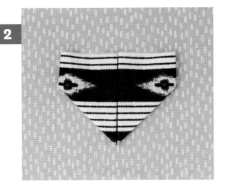

2

Holding the middle of the upper edge, fold each half down the vertical centerline of the napkin.

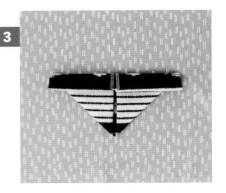

3

Fold the lower edge of each tail up to meet the base of the triangle, then fold one more time, so there is a band across the base of the triangle.

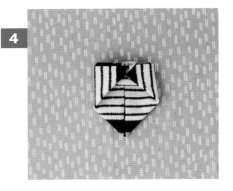

4

Fold the right side over to the left, using one-third of the width of the napkin. Then fold the left side over, tucking it behind the top layer to secure it.

5

Arrange on the plate with the point facing up.

TRIANGLE

Lay the napkin out as a square with the finished side facing down, then fold the napkin into three equal parts, forming a horizontal rectangle.

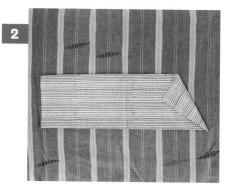

Fold the upper right corner down toward the left, forming a point at the lower right corner.

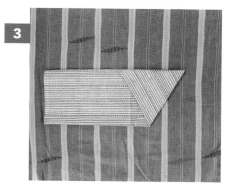

Fold the angled right edge up to the upper edge, forming a triangle on top of the napkin.

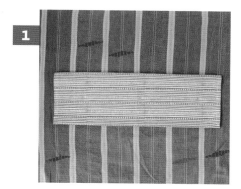

Then fold again, forming another triangle.

Fold the lower corner up toward the right, then tuck the point under the top layer of the triangle to secure it.

Arrange a napkin at each place setting, or stack at a buffet.

WAVE

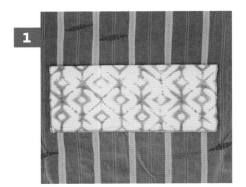

1

Lay the napkin out as a square, with the finished side facing down, then fold the napkin in to three equal parts towards the center, forming a horizontal rectangle.

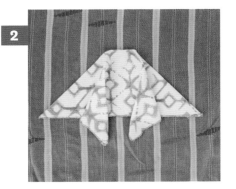

2

Lift the top layer of the upper right corner and fold it towards the the inside of the napkin to the vertical centerline, and then repeat with the left, forming four triangular flaps.

3

Fold in half so all the points meet on one side. Then, holding the bottom point, fan out four layers of points at the upper right side.

4

Lay the napkin on the plate, points to the right. Then insert the flatware and fold the points over and to the left of the plate wrapping around the flatware.

5

Arrange on the plate.

FLOWER

1

Lay the napkin out as a square, with the finished side facing down, then fold each corner into the center of the napkin, forming a diamond.

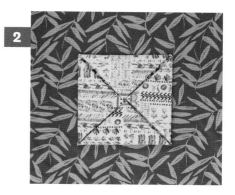

2

Then fold each point toward the center again, forming a square.

3

Flip the napkin over, and fold all four corners in toward the center, forming a diamond.

4

Holding the center of the diamond, reach underneath each point and gently pull the edge out to form a petal.

5

Adjust the petals for symmetry, then place in the center of the plate.

planning the get-together

PLAN THE TABLE

I always start by planning with the table first, because that is where we'll spend most of our time during a gathering. The remaining pieces will make up the rest of the night and help you plan accordingly for the preparation so you can enjoy yourself the day of.

PLAN THE MENU

Bohemianism translated to the plate incorporates a few core characteristics: seasonal ingredients, reasonably easy to put together, and full of flavor to inspire conversations and memories. Remember, this is about memory-making, not a Michelin star. Sometimes the tastiest food is the simplest, so long as you use fresh and seasonal ingredients.

When planning your menu, suit your own strengths. The gathering is about good people and good food, which means you don't have to make it all by hand. Choose the recipes that you enjoy preparing, and leave the rest to premade goodies or takeout. When deciding what foods to include, be democratic and choose items that appeal to most people and are not finicky in their preparation. Consider your guests' diets and preferences when selecting your menu, ensuring you offer a good, healthy spread of options in different food groups so no one goes hungry based on their allergies or lifestyle.

To determine how much food and drink to plan for each person, stick to this helpful guide for each course:

Course	Servings per person
Cocktails	2 drinks per hour
Appetizers	8 to 12 appetizers per person
Main Dish	6 oz. per person
Wine	half a bottle for each guest
Side Dishes	2 to 4 oz. per person
Dessert	1 piece per person, or 5 oz. of ice cream

PLAN THE GUEST LIST AND INVITATIONS

Two weeks prior to your gathering is just enough time to send out paper invitations. Formal events demand a more sophisticated invitation, but you can keep the wording simple and inviting like the examples shown here.

Paper invitations are a wonderful tool for pre-planned events, but in this modern, tech-savvy world there are a few more options that can help you to save time on prep and ensure more timely RSVPs. Email-based invites or Facebook events are common and effective for most guests. Group texts can get a little tricky, as some people do not understand the concept of not replying to all. Individual text messages or emails are a good common ground to save on time but still connect personally with your guests. Remember, it is about freedom and enjoyment, and with that comes spontaneity. If you train yourself to believe it is not a real get-together without a paper invite, you'll miss out on hosting a lot of fun evenings.

A quick thank-you note, call, or text after the event to your guests (or, if you are a guest, to the hostess) is a nice, impressive gesture. We are not too busy to appreciate our people.

PLAN THE NIGHT

The second you decide on hosting, plan the decor and menu. In addition to deciding what to cook, look at the prep time for each item and plan a backwards timeline from the hour you invite people to arrive to the first item that needs to be cooked. All fresh ingredients can be prepped the night before and cooked in the morning. If possible, it's ideal to cook everything the day of for freshness, but you can spend the night before washing, prepping, and chopping all the ingredients so you can simply whip it together the next day.

You can also set the table the night before, adding just the fresh or organic decor the next day. I stack all of the pieces on the table the night before, including servingware, with a little sticky note on each piece to help me (and any helper) know what goes in each. I like to set the table right before guests arrive, because it is a way for me to relax and meditate a bit before the guests swarm. Setting the table is one of the more simple tasks for me, but you might find other tasks come easier, and those can be the last things you do before guests arrive.

PLAN THE FLORALS

Florals are both a classic and modern way to make a special statement for any occasion. But they don't have to be complex works of art to be special. Florals are not just for the table—they can brighten any room your guests will be sharing. Here are the most common ways anyone can bring fresh and organic vibes to any setting:

- small plants
- store-bought arrangement-turned-centerpiece
- greenery on the table
- bud vases
- wildflowers/other adornments from outside
- dried flowers for reuse

Almost anything can be made into a vase for your floral arrangements. If it does not hold water, simply insert a plastic or glass container, or even a reusable food storage bag.

Floral Arranging Tips

- Use florals that are as fresh as possible. If you are foraging, collect florals in the morning when their water content is highest. If you are purchasing, look for crisp bright green stems; the blooms should be perky and the petals free from dark edges. Don't select stems with closed buds, as they often never open all the way (with the exception of lilies, tulips, and gladiolas).

- Trim the florals to take in the most water. Remove all of the leaves that will be under the water line, placing the florals in lukewarm water as soon as possible. Stems should be cut on the diagonal to increase the surface area soaking up the water. Woody stems can be hammered or broken for better water intake.

- Picture an imaginary outline as your arrangement shape. Begin by placing the basic outline greenery and then add in stems, considering height and color, while picturing a basic outline shape of the entire arrangement. Knowing when to stop is vital, and learned over time. Don't try too hard, or the florals will look like old-timely funeral arrangements. Bright colors make bold statements, and irregularity can add interest and charm. The most important factor for your arrangement is to repeat the natural, organic line and form of the flowers.

For seamless party planning, see the party planning sheet in the back of the book (page 223).

the bar

Two drinks per hour per person is a loose rule to plan by, but the true amount of liquor needed depends on the type of party, the length of the event, and what type of food you will be serving. Obviously, a cocktail party with light snacks means there is more time to consume the libations, while a formal dinner leaves less time for cocktails and more time for wine paired with your courses. The bar setup, like the table setting and buffet table, should be easy to use and invite people to feel comfortable with an old classic, or to explore a new twist. For small dinner parties, set up beverage supplies on a cart, small table, or counter and either let it be self-serve or serve it yourself as the host. Place the bar at the center of the party for easy service, or away from the crowd in a non-congested area of the party.

As far as cocktail napkins, paper napkins can go quickly—plan for two to three per person. Guests are more likely to hold onto a cloth cocktail napkin for several servings through the night. Having a unique array of napkin designs can also allow them to serve as an informal name tag, so guests can always keep an eye on their glass.

Commercially purchased ice makes for a fresher-tasting drink than the ice from your freezer, which could be tainted by frozen food. If you are mainly serving cocktails, plan for ¾ to 1 pound of ice per guest. No need for fancy ice chests or buckets—anything can become a chilled container if first lined with plastic and then aluminum foil to keep it chilled.

You'll want a well-stocked bar of all the classics. Geographical or seasonal factors may call for a few unique add-ons, but the chart shown here is a good base to go by.

Type of Drink	Number of Servings
bottle of wine (750 milliliters)	four 6-oz. drinks
bottle of liquor (750 milliliters)	seventeen 1½-oz. drinks
bottle of mixer (10 ounces)	ten 1-oz. drinks
bottle of champagne (750 milliliters)	5 servings
case of champagne	30 servings
keg of beer	130 to 140 servings
gallon of punch	24 servings

This chart will get your home bar ready for any cocktail that comes your way. That said, you may way to ease into this set-up as you get more aquainted with different cocktails, particularly in the liquor category.

Liquor	Wine	Liqueur	Beer	Mixers	Garnish
VODKA: 2 bottles	**WHITE WINE:** 4 bottles	**AMARETTO:** 1 bottle	*Two six packs	**SPARKLING WATER:** 6 bottles	Lemon
SCOTCH: 2 bottles	**RED WINE:** 4 bottles	**APEROL:** 1 bottle	**LAGER:** pale lager light lager pilsner amber lager bock dark lager	**CLUB SODA:** 6 bottles	Lime
LIGHT RUM: 2 bottles	**ROSÉ:** 2 bottles	**CAMPARI:** 1 bottle		**TONIC WATER:** 2 bottles	Orange
DARK RUM: 2 bottles	**DRY VERMOUTH:** 1 bottle	**COINTREAU:** 1 bottle	**ALE:** wheat beer pale ale bitter amber ale stout porter blonde ale saison	**GINGER ALE:** 2 bottles	Bitters
GIN: 2 bottles	**SWEET VERMOUTH:** 1 bottle	**FERNET-BRANCA:** 1 bottle		**COKE:** 2 bottles	Maraschino cherries
BOURBON: 2 bottles	**CHAMPAGNE:** 4 bottles	**KAHLUA:** 1 bottle		**SIMPLE SYRUP:** 1 bottle	Olives
WHISKEY: 2 bottles		**ST-GERMAIN:** 1 bottle			Mint
					Salt and sugar

FOR AN OLD-FASHIONED ROCKS GLASS:

Negroni

1 oz gin

1 oz sweet vermouth

1 oz Campari

Orange wedge

Combine all the ingredients in an old-fashioned glass with a large ice cube. Stir until chilled. Squeeze and garnish with an orange wedge.

FOR A HIGHBALL GLASS:

Paloma

2 oz tequila or mezcal

2 oz club soda

2 oz grapefruit juice

½ oz lime juice

1 dash sugar

Grapefruit wedge (optional)

Combine all the ingredients in a shaker or measuring cup with ice. Strain into a chilled highball glass with a salted rim, filled with ice. Garnish with a grapefruit wedge.

FOR A COCKTAIL/ MARTINI/COUPE GLASS:

Harrington

1½ oz vodka

¼ oz triple sec

¼ oz chartreuse

Orange peel (optional)

Combine all the ingredients in a shaker or measuring cup with ice, and strain into a chilled cocktail glass. Garnish with an orange peel.

FOR A CHAMPAGNE FLUTE:

Classic Champagne Cocktail

Champagne

2 to 3 dashes Angostura bitters

1 sugar cube

Lemon twist (optional)

Place the sugar cube in the flute, add 2 or 3 dashes of bitters, and fill the glass with champagne. Garnish with a lemon twist.

FOR A WINE GLASS:

Venetian Spritz

3 oz prosecco

2 oz Aperol or Campari

1 oz sparkling water

Orange slice (optional)

Combine all the ingredients in a chilled glass with ice. Stir and garnish with an orange slice.

FOR A PILSNER GLASS:

Beer Bee's Knees

3 oz hefeweizen

1½ oz gin

1 oz lemon juice

1 oz honey syrup

(1:1 mix of honey and water shaken together)

Lemon wedge (optional)

Combine the gin, lemon juice, and honey syrup in a shaker filled with ice. Shake vigorously and strain into pilsner glass without ice. Pour the beer over the mixture. Garnish with lemon.

You can maximize magic in the mundane through small details and personal touches.

party ideas *through the* seasons

The themed party ideas you'll find in the following pages guide you through entertaining for all of the seasons of the year. For these ideas, you'll mainly use pieces from your collection, with small handmade additions or items found at flea markets, while traveling, or from around the house. The focus of every get-together is about the company—never a large budget or perfectly catered meal. Remember, you can maximize magic in the mundane through small details and personal touches.

Season
fall

F ALL IS THE PERFECT SEASON TO INVITE friends over for community. With summer over, everyone is getting set back into their routines and looking for a reason to spend time out in the perfect cooler evenings. These parties are all based around shareable meals, meant to be enjoyed with a lively conversation about your latest adventures or your favorite team's chances.

harvest party

There is nothing better than vegetables grown in your own garden. Whether from a pot on the back patio or the full side yard, homegrown produce is always worth the fuss. And tomatoes are generally the easiest gateway plant. When my husband started gardening years ago, he ruined all store-bought tomatoes for me. So August through September, I eat my fill.

My enthusiasm for tomatoes is matched by his enthusiasm for gardening, so our little crop can usually feed our family, neighbors, coworkers, and pretty much anyone we meet during that season who even remotely likes vegetables. We cap off the end of the season by cooking up all the tomatoes to share with friends. Tomatoes are in nearly all the dishes and adorn the table, bar, and every flat space. At the end of the night, we wrap up a small crop for everyone to take home, along with a bunch of herbs that we trimmed and dried earlier in the summer.

Pasta is always an easy, quick dinner party meal, which leaves time to make a few different sauces to please all tastes.

— MENU —

Appetizers

MARINATED OLIVES, BRUSCHETTA (THREE WAYS)

Main Dishes

ARRABBIATA SAUCE*, PESTO SAUCE, ROASTED TOMATOES, PASTA (THREE TYPES OF NOODLES), GARDEN GREEN SALAD, ROASTED ZUCCHINI + PEPPERS + CAULIFLOWER

Wine Pairing

A MIX OF ITALIAN TUSCAN REDS (CHIANTI, SANGIOVESE, BARBERA, MONTEPULCIANO), PINOT GRIGIO, PROSECCO

Cocktail

CAMPARI SPRITZ* AND NEGRONI*

Dessert

PANNA COTTA WITH FRESH BERRIES

*RECIPES FOLLOW

arrabbiata sauce

This traditional, spicy take on marinara is the perfect way to complement rich wine and savory, buttery pasta.

SERVES 8

½ cup extra-virgin olive oil

2 medium yellow onions, minced

12 cloves garlic, minced

3 tablespoons red pepper flakes

4 28-oz cans San Marzano Tomatoes, whole

2 bay leaves

Kosher sea salt to taste

Large bunch fresh basil

Heat the olive oil in a large pan and sauté the onion with a pinch of salt until translucent, about 10 minutes. Add the garlic and red pepper flakes and cook until fragrant, about 1 to 2 minutes.

In a large bowl, crush the tomatoes with your hands, leaving a few large pieces. Transfer the tomatoes to the pan, and bring to a simmer. Add the bay leaves and partially cover with a lid.

Allow the sauce to simmer for at least 35 minutes, checking occasionally to make sure the tomatoes do not burn. Turn off the heat and season to your taste with salt. Stir in the fresh basil leaves. Finish with a drizzle of olive oil and serve over pasta, meats, or hard bread.

campari spritz and negroni

This refreshing pair of drinks is not only gorgeous but easy to mix, with just four ingredients in each one.

campari spritz

3 oz prosecco

2 oz Campari

1 oz sparkling water

Orange slice

Combine all the ingredients in a chilled glass with ice. Stir and garnish with an orange slice.

negroni

1 oz Campari

1 oz gin

1 oz semi-sweet vermouth

Orange peel

Combine Campari, gin, and vermouth in a shaker to combine. Run the orange peel around the rim of the glass. Pour the cocktail over ice and garnish with the orange peel.

Aperitivo is the magical practice of pre-meal bubbles to stimulate your appetite and ready the stomach for a good meal. Light, refreshing, and fizzy, these concoctions consist of a complex liqueur and a dash of sparkling or soda water over ice, typically with a fruit garnish, so they look good and taste good.

This dinner party utilizes:

- White dinner plates
- White salad plates
- Gold flatware
- Water glasses
- Red wine glasses
- Bread basket

Table Design Note

To create height with the centerpiece, I used some serving platters and bowls in which to group the tomatoes. I also layered some spinach from the garden underneath some of the tomatoes to add some extra color.

additions to the table

With multiple wines for everyone to sample, I want a way to easily pass the bottles and load them into a wine caddy. Guests can choose their poison and easily read the label to remember their favorites.

For name cards, I use my trusty acrylic cards, with sticker letters, laid across a thrifted bathroom tile to add earthy texture and remind everyone of the earthiness of the dinner.

Highball glasses are a great shape to showcase your pre-dinner spritzes and negronis. Skinny, tall glasses also up less room on a packed dinner table.

Because Italian food calls for all the wine, I add a white wine glass, choosing a handmade green goblet to add a punch of color. To add some texture to the table, I use vintage rattan cup holders to hold the water glasses.

Shibori-dyed napkins are a simple DIY that can add a great pop of color to any tabletop. You can order pre-finished dinner napkins and use the process described in the following DIY (page 72).

I add an unused terra cotta–pot saucer to turn the normal dinner plate into a pasta bowl, making sure all of the noodles stay on the plate.

how to dye your own napkins

Hand-dyed napkins are an excellent way to contribute a handmade and thoughtful item to your dinner table that does not require too much time or creativity. Plus, it's a fun outdoor craft that you can complete in just a few hours.

There are a variety of natural and homemade dye combinations that you can geek out over, but going through those options would be a book in itself. For the benefit of time, we'll use a store-bought dye to quickly transform your linens.

YOU WILL NEED:

1 package of finished white cotton napkins (usually comes in a set of 12)

Rubber bands, clips, tape, etc. to create a resist

1 bottle of dye in the color of your choice—or more if you want to create a two-toned or other colorful design

1 large bucket that can hold at least 2 gallons of liquid

Spoon, chopstick, or other utensil to stir and scoop in the dye

1 cup white vinegar*

1 cup salt*

Rubber gloves

Old towels or paper towels to clean up the mess

Flattened cardboard box

Drying rack or ladder to dry linens on

*For non-natural fibers, use vinegar, not salt. For natural fibers, use salt, not vinegar. See step 3.**

1. **Prepare the fabric for dying.** Throw all the napkins or fabric into the washing machine to remove any finishes applied commercially. Dry according to the care label.

2. **Tie up the fabric to create patterns.** Using rubber bands, clips, tape, and any number of different tools, fold and tie the fabric. This will create different patterns on the fabric by preventing the dye from soaking into every crease.

3. **Prep the dye.** Fill your bucket three-quarters full with warm water. If your item is made from a non-natural fiber, such as polyester or rayon, add one cup of white vinegar. For a natural fiber, such as cotton or silk, add one cup of salt. Add the dye, either the full powder package or half of the liquid bottle, and stir.

4. **Ready to dip.** When you're ready to dye, completely wet the fabric with warm water in a separate bucket or in the sink. Squeeze to extract excess water, then gently drop the linen into the dye and poke down with a spoon so that every part is covered in dye. Let the linen sit in the dye for at least 30 minutes, stirring occasionally to flip the linen so it is fully covered in dye.

5. **Remove your linens.** Using two utensils or your gloved hand, carefully lift the linen out of the bucket and place on the flattened cardboard, and let dry in the sun.

6. **Unfold the design.** Once it is no longer sopping, undo the clips, bands or other accessories to unfold the linen completely. Drape across the drying rack or ladder and continue to dry in the sun.

7. **Set the dye.** Once the linens have completely dried in the sun, run them through the washing machine and dryer, or hand-wash and hang in the sun to set the dye. If you have done sets of napkins in multiple colors, wash each color separately for this first wash.

Shibori is the ancient Japanese technique of binding, folding, twisting, compressing, or stitching cloth to create a resist in your dying, which results in a pattern with areas the dye hasn't reached. Traditionally, binding is done with thread, but today we can use a number of different modern accessories to create interesting resist patterns.

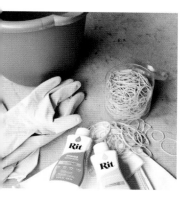

pattern ideas

Shown here are finished napkins with their bundled, undyed partners. Use the images as a reference to create a similar look, or experiment on your own to create new patterns.

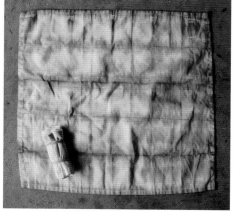

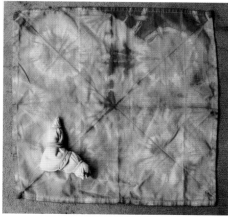

taco bar fiesta

Taco Tuesday is not just a trendy hashtag but a way of life. Tacos are not only one of the most perfect food items, but they're also pretty easy to prepare and share with friends.

Taco bars are my old faithful party menu. Even through college, when you really don't spend any time in the kitchen—and party food is generally prepped in a large drink bucket or as Jell-O shots—it was never too much trouble to buy all the ingredients and prep the bar. I would man the grill and my roommates would chop vegetables. We would set up the kitchen buffet-style, then all gather around the tile-topped table my mom made to fit our tiny, brightly painted dining room. These days, with maturing tastes and personalities, a taco bar is a bit fancier, but the fun is still the same.

This is the perfect dinner party to throw when you don't have a ton of time to cook. Most of the time is spent prepping ingredients, with the only real cooking done on the grill. Even the cocktails can be prepped in large batches. You can also offer a multitude of different toppings and fillings to please everyone's diet and lifestyle.

MENU

Taco Bar Setup

QUICK-PICKLED ONIONS*, LIME WEDGES, CHOPPED CILANTRO, GRILLED CORN, GUACAMOLE*, CHOPPED TOMATOES, PICKLED AND CHOPPED JALAPEÑOS, QUESO FRESCO, GRILLED TORTILLAS, GRILLED AND MARINATED FLANK STEAK, GRILLED AND MARINATED CHICKEN THIGHS, GRILLED JACKFRUIT

Cocktail

MARGARITA AND MEZCAL MULE*

Dessert

CHURROS

*RECIPES FOLLOW

quick-pickled onions

A quick handmade topping that you can keep on hand for long after the party.

MAKES 2 TO 3 CUPS

2 red onions, thinly sliced

1½ cups apple cider vinegar

⅔ cup water

3 tablespoons sugar

2 teaspoons kosher salt

Place the onions in a jar or cup. In a bowl, whisk together the vinegar, water, sugar, and salt until the sugar and salt dissolve. Pour over the sliced onions. Let sit at room temperature for 1 hour.

guacamole

Guacamole can be an art form, but this classically simple recipe will be the perfect party pleaser.

MAKES 4 TO 6 CUPS

6 avocados, chopped

2 jalapeños, seeded and diced

½ cup diced sweet onion

½ cup fresh cilantro, chopped

2 limes, juiced

½ teaspoon kosher salt

½ teaspoon pepper

In a bowl, mash the avocado with a fork. Stir in the peppers, onion, cilantro, lime juice, salt, and pepper. Mix until combined to desired consistency. Taste and season, adding more salt, pepper, or lime juice as needed.

You can make the pickled onions and guacamole ahead of time and store in the fridge in a sealed container or jar. To keep the guac from browning, keep the avocado pits in the bowl.

mezcal mule

1½ ounces mezcal

1½ ounces guava juice

1 ounce chilled ginger beer

Sliced lime

Muddle a handful of ice cubes in your shaker. Fill a tall glass or Moscow mule mug with the muddled ice, then add the mezcal and guava juice. Top with ginger beer and a squeeze of lime. Garnish with lime slices and serve.

This dinner
party utilizes:

- White dinner plates
- Wooden bowls
- Wooden flatware
- Water glasses
- Colored glassware

Table Design Notes

With trips already happening back and forth to the taco bar, have pitchers of water and margaritas on the table to decrease trips and keep your guests at the table.

Recognizing your guests' favorite toppings, you can scoop those up and add to the table for easy access as well.

additions to the table

I strung some paper flags and picado across the backyard to signify a special occasion. These Mexican folk-art crafts are commonly displayed for celebrations of all kinds. These are made of tissue paper, but you can find reusable plastic flags that can be used time and again for different parties.

To make it easier for guests to grab and go, I wrapped each taco type in foil with a washi-tape label. This is a great way to keep food from cross-contaminating if there are allergies, and it can keep the tacos warm if you prep them earlier in the day.

In place of name tags, I found these Mexican milagros to nestle into each place setting. This unique touch not only adds a bit of charm to the table, it is a fun take-home item for all the guests.

These napkins were a flea market find and feature different Central American origins, with coordinating stitching and colors to make a new set that can be added to over time. These are luncheon-sized napkins, so they don't take up too much space in the place setting, but they're just big enough to wipe up after tacos.

To avoid spending money or time on a centerpiece, I gathered small plants from around the house and from my mom's kitchen to create a festive line of cacti down the center of the table.

Cacti are a great centerpiece because they don't waterfall over onto the table or onto the plates and are a low height, so everyone can chat across the table with their neighbors.

moroccan tapas party

When you mention "bohemian," most people picture a Moroccan riad filled with chunky textiles, colorful tile, low seating, daybeds, and intricately patterned glassware, carvings, and bone inlays. These courtyard settings represent many of the bohemian design principles—interesting, organic, layered—and are the perfect relaxing oasis to retreat from everyday chaos. But unfortunately, we cannot all jump on a plane to escape to these heavenly spaces, so this party focuses on bringing that vibe into your own home.

With a snack-focused dinner, guests can graze from lounge to lounge and just relax into conversation. This casual setting lends to casual dishes, all of which you could buy pre-prepared at the deli, or make a few dishes each day and store away for the party.

MENU

Tapas Dinner Setup

MARINATED OLIVES, OLIVE TAPENADE, ROASTED ALMONDS, HARISSA PASTE, MOROCCAN-SPICED CHICKPEAS*, MARINATED CHICKEN SKEWERS, LAMB MEATBALLS, TABBOULEH, COUSCOUS WITH ROASTED VEGETABLES, BAGUETTE SLICES

Cocktail

MOROCCAN MINT TEA JULEP*

Dessert

RICE PUDDING WITH POMEGRANATE-SEED TOPPING

*RECIPES FOLLOW

moroccan-spiced chickpeas

These are the perfect salty snack to pair with all the other tapas-styled dishes. The balance of salty, sweet, and crunchy . . . be prepared to refill often.

MAKES 1½ CUPS

2 15½-ounce cans chickpeas, drained and rinsed

2 tablespoons olive oil

1 teaspoon ground cumin

½ teaspoon cayenne

½ teaspoon ground cinnamon

½ teaspoon garlic powder

¼ teaspoon paprika

½ teaspoon kosher salt

Preheat the oven to 400°F. Line a baking sheet with parchment paper. Pat the chickpeas dry and place them on the baking sheet. Drizzle with olive oil, then roast in the oven for 40 to 45 minutes, tossing every 10 to 15 minutes.

Combine the spices in a medium bowl. When the chickpeas are golden, dry, and crunchy, remove from the oven and toss with the spice blend.

moroccan mint tea julep

Moroccan Mint tea is a treat all on its own, but with the addition of bourbon, you'll have a tasty, sweet cocktail to complement the spicy toppings on some of the tapas dishes.

YIELDS 1 DRINK

1 Moroccan mint tea bag

3 to 5 fresh mint leaves

1 ounce simple syrup

2 ounces bourbon

Bring water to boil and steep the tea bag for 8 minutes. Pour the hot tea over ice and chill until ready to use. To serve, place mint leaves in the bottom of a highball glass and muddle. Add simple syrup, bourbon, and 4 ounces of tea. Top with ice and garnish with mint.

This dinner party utilizes:

- Assorted servingware and baskets
- Assorted fruit and condiment bowls
- Assorted small serving utensils
- Assorted side plates
- Drink carafe
- Tall tumbler glasses
- Wooden boards
- Small tables
- Pillows and rugs from around the house
- Indoor chairs, furniture, and outdoor furniture

Table Design Notes

When putting together a community table like this one, cake stands are your best friend in creating height so you can add as many small dishes as possible. You can also flip over bowls or other household items to create pedestals. Worried that your dish may slide off? Use double-sided tape or large tape donuts to give the dish just a loose attachment to the table—that should be enough to keep it in place if it gets bumped.

additions to the table

Though not needed for the food selections or traditional theme, I add some flatware throughout the tables, thinking about my guests' comfort. Some people don't love to get their hands messy!

My secret weapon for this type of setup is army cots. They fold up nicely for storage and are sturdy enough to seat three to four guests. You can find vintage cots in neutral or green canvas at antique stores, thrift stores, and on Craigslist at a really good price. You can also easily replace the canvas with a few seams on the sewing machine.

Throws and pillows make for a cozy environment, perfect for this more intimate kind of gathering.

When purchasing side plates, do so with the types of parties you'd like to throw in mind. I bought these Tunisian plates in green and turquoise with the intention of using them in gatherings just like this one.

I included Moroccan-style lanterns throughout the seating areas and walkways to add ambiance.

Moroccan style is a conglomeration of Asian, European, Middle Eastern, and African influences, making it a cultural crucible where drastically different elements intermingle and create opulent and timeless beauty. Moroccan dining traditions can vary, but for this type of communal eating, a few traditions seem natural to include.

- Flatware is rarely used. Instead, opt for bread or your hands to scoop and snack.

- Separate dishes into several small servings scattered across the table so that everyone can reach what they would like without reaching across someone or having to pass a large plate.

- Cookware and serveware are often made of differing materials than those you find in a typical Western kitchen. But the traditional earthenware, woven baskets, and brass trays are an easy transition from kitchen to service for a beautiful display.

- Tea is a necessity for etiquette and digestion, but the night is often capped with espresso or lattes.

- Scented water dispensers, typically with orange flower or rose water, are spread throughout the party to freshen hands before and after eating, while also adding a decor element to each service area.

gratitude-filled thanksgiving

The holidays offer the ultimate entertaining events, as all of your people gather in one place to slow down and reflect on the year behind them and the one in front of them.

There are so many decor options that can bring the fall spirit indoors, and you'll find several variations are combined in the holiday section later in this book. For this party, I wanted to focus on the classic pieces in your collection, paired with a new tradition you can adopt in your family to preserve all of the memories you are grateful for.

This table features a handmade journal, in which each guest can write what they are most thankful and grateful for. Next year, pull them out and pass them around—to the same guests or new ones—and continue to collect those things which your most loved people are most thankful for with each passing year.

MENU

Appetizers

BUTTERNUT SQUASH CROSTINI, MAPLE PECANS, GLAZED WALNUTS WITH BLUE CHEESE, BACON, FENNEL, AND APPLE CHUTNEY WITH BAGUETTE SLICES

Main Dishes

ROASTED BRUSSELS SPROUTS, GARLIC MUSHROOMS*, BRAISED GREENS, POTATO GRATIN, MIXED GRAIN STUFFING, SPATCHCOCK WHOLE TURKEY

Wine Pairing

HEAVY RED WINE (SHIRAZ, MERLOT, MALBEC)

Cocktail

CHAMPAGNE PUNCH*

Dessert

CRANBERRY TART

*RECIPES FOLLOW

garlic mushrooms

These are my favorite vegetables for the holidays. Slightly decadent
with all that butter, but sure to make even the mushroom-haters happy.

SERVES 12

3 pounds mushrooms
(cremini or white)

6 tablespoons capers

12 large cloves garlic

3 tablespoons extra-virgin olive oil

Salt and pepper to taste

1 stick (8 tablespoons) salted butter,
cut into small cubes

2 lemons, juiced

1 cup chopped flat-leaf parsley

Preheat the oven to 450°F. Cut the mushrooms in half and toss with capers,
garlic, oil, salt, and pepper in a shallow baking dish.

Sprinkle the cubes of butter over the pan and roast until the mushrooms
are tender and the butter sauce thickens, 18 to 25 minutes.

Top with the lemon juice and toss with the parsley to serve.

champagne punch

Just the right amount of fancy in a shareable serving.

SERVES 12

1 cup triple sec

1 cup brandy

½ cup Chambord

2 cups unsweetened pineapple juice

4 cups chilled ginger ale

2 chilled 750-ml bottles dry champagne

Ice

In a bowl combine triple sec, brandy, Chambord, and pineapple juice. Cover and chill the mixture for at least 4 hours, or overnight. In a large punch bowl, combine the chilled mixture with ginger ale and champagne. Add ice.

When there is a lot going on in the kitchen, batched cocktails or punches are the perfect pairing for the hectic menu. You don't necessarily need a punch bowl; you can also use a large pitcher or drink dispenser. Punch bowls store relatively well, as you can store all of their petite glasses inside the bowl.

This dinner party utilizes:

- White dinner plate
- White salad plate
- Wine glasses
- Gold flatware

Table Design Notes

Candles are the perfect touch for any type of gathering. When choosing candles, base your decision on burn rate, rather than price. Some candles melt too quickly and need to be replaced throughout the night, so you might as well invest in a slower-burning wax.

If the base of the candle is too big for the candle holder you have selected, trim it down with scissors or soften it in hot water so it is malleable. If the candle end is too small, wrap a piece of plastic wrap around it and wedge it into the holder.

Make sure to take a moment when everyone is seated—the candles lit, the food all prepared and ready for feasting—to look around and take it all in. Save that memory, that warm feeling, and remember that all of your work to get to the table was to share quality time with those seated with you.

additions to the table

A long, draping table runner is a great way to add instant elegance to the table. This one is a simple silk chiffon fabric, casually laid down the center of the table. When measuring the fabric, add three to four yards to the measurement of the table to create a pooling effect.

My favorite decor is that which I can get a lot of use out of. Dried greenery is an option that can provide a great touch to so many tabletop designs. These eucalyptus leaves are dyed gold. You can buy dried eucalyptus stems in assorted colors, or natural, for about the same price as fresh, but they last much longer.

I collected assorted mid-century highball glasses with metallic accents to serve as the water glasses for this table. They add a special touch to the table and are a fun item to collect that can serve several different party themes and cocktail choices.

I utilize my reusable nametags. When it comes to holidays, you are likely to have the same guests in attendance year after year, so if you are going to invest in something special, these nametags are a safe bet. If you select a neutral design, like these modern sticker place cards, you can reuse them for parties and years to come.

When you are trying to decide what type of candle holders to keep on hand, here is a tip: brass will never go out of style and is easy to find. You can find similar designs or mix and match shapes and heights, like those shown here.

thanksgiving variations

Most people get their first dose of entertaining when preparing for a holiday meal. This section shows you six different table setups using your collection pieces, along with a few affordable additions that you can reuse in different ways throughout the years.

These grouped-decor centerpieces are a great way to prepare for a family-style setup. Even if everyone serves up at the buffet, you might need a few things to share across the table, and these groupings leave plenty of space for that.

The plain round coaster can be presented several ways as a name card if you get creative with the placement of the text. The difference between this setup and the previous is as simple as switching the napkins and name cards and spreading out of the center decor.

101

Focusing on three different colors and paring down the decor to larger pieces makes the style more modern. For each place card, I cut a strip of paper and folded it in half at an angle.

Similar to the previous setting, decreasing the range of colors and textures can make the setting more modern. This setup keeps things simple, but texture keeps it interesting. These gauze napkins are just trimmed pieces from an old table runner—no sewing necessary.

When building up your collection of table decor, consider things you can use in multiple ways through the years—one year nestled into the centerpiece, and the next styled in each place setting.

Placing all decor in a basket with a few greens keeps cleanup quick and easy. This place setting also includes additional name cards in the wine glasses.

season

winter

IN ADDITION TO THE HOLIDAY SEASON, winter offers many occasions to tuck indoors and gather with friends. This season's parties are all about enjoying rich food and drink, while creating cozy scenes so that no one will want to leave the warmth of the home and conversation.

colorful, modern christmas dinner

The holiday season is packed with traditions, but not at every turn. For this setup, I combined a mix of modern colors with classic decor pieces for a fresh table design.

For years we always stuck with the classic dinner choices of turkey or ham, but once we ventured over to this traditional Italian pork roast, we never looked back. I first tasted porchetta at a market in Rome. After one bite of that salty, crunchy skin, I began searching for a recipe to replicate that same simple taste, and I've gotten pretty close with this one. The secret to achieving that perfectly crispy skin is to let it sit in the fridge and dry out after seasoning and before roasting. Each time we cook this meal, we play with the mixture of spices, making small tweaks. When shared with friends and family, we get to learn which combos they prefer too, making it a truly customized family recipe.

MENU

Appetizers

STUFFED MUSHROOMS, ROSEMARY-CARAMEL POPCORN, ARTICHOKE PATE WITH BAGUETTE SLICES

Main Dishes

ITALIAN GREEN BEANS WITH PANCETTA, LEEK GRATIN, BUTTERNUT SQUASH AND APPLE PUREE, PORCHETTA*, BLACK PEPPER DINNER ROLLS

Wine Pairing

LIGHT, UNSWEET WHITE (SAUVIGNON BLANC, ALBARIÑO, CHARDONNAY)

Cocktail

HOT CIDER TODDY*

Dessert

CREAM PUFFS

*RECIPES FOLLOW

hot cider toddy

The sweetness of this cocktail is the perfect pair for the salty main dish.

SERVES 4

4 cups fresh apple cider

8 cloves

2 cinnamon sticks

4 whole star anise

¼ cup honey

2 tablespoons fresh lemon juice

1 cup whiskey

Lemon and apple slices (optional)

Combine the apple cider, cloves cinnamon sticks, and star anise in a saucepan and bring to a boil. Turn off the heat, cover with a lid, and allow to steep for 15 minutes. Remove the cinnamon sticks, cloves, and star anise. Add the honey and stir until dissolved. Add the whisky and lemon juice and stir to combine.

Divide into four mugs and garnish each with a cinnamon stick, lemon slice, apple slice, and star anise as desired.

porchetta

By wrapping your own roast, you are sure to have the perfect balance of lean and fatty meats in every delicious bite.

SERVES 12 TO 15

2 tablespoons fennel seeds

2 tablespoons crushed red pepper flakes

2 tablespoons minced fresh sage

1 tablespoon minced fresh rosemary

6 cloves garlic, chopped

1 5- to 6-pound piece fresh pork belly, skin on

Kosher salt, to taste

1 trimmed 2- 3-pound boneless, center-cut pork loin

Half an orange, seeded and thinly sliced

Cotton twine

Toast the fennel seeds and red pepper flakes in a small skillet over medium heat until fragrant, 1 to 2 minutes. Let the spices cool, and then grind and transfer them to a bowl, along with the sage, rosemary, and garlic.

Place the pork belly skin-side up and score diagonally in a checkerboard pattern. Flip it over and poke several holes through the skin randomly, all over the belly.

Generously salt both the belly and loin and rub both with the fennel mixture. Arrange the loin in the center of the belly and top with the orange slices. Roll the belly around the loin so the ends meet, and then use cotton twine to tie around the roll in two or three places. Transfer the roast to a wire rack set on a rimmed baking sheet. Chill in the fridge for 4 hours, or overnight.

Preheat the oven to 500°F. Season the outside of the roast with salt and roast for 40 minutes. Reduce the heat to 300°F and continue roasting, rotating the pan and turning the porchetta occasionally until an instant-read thermometer inserted in the center of the meat registers 145°F, about 1½ to 2 hours.

Let rest for 30 minutes, then slice with a serrated knife into ½-inch rounds to serve.

This dinner party utilizes:

- White dinner plates
- White salad plates
- Wine glasses
- Gold flatware

Table Design Note

For formal tables, leave 24 inches for each guest at the table. You can squeeze closer and closer together as formality falls away, but always leave space for each person to comfortably bend their elbows and eat their meal.

As the years go by, you will likely pick up a few children around the table. Including a few magical surprises for them throughout the night and on the table is a way to bring them in on the magic of the moment. For small children, I nestle small deer in the trees as a hide-and-seek game for the kids. I also have paint and markers waiting for after dinner so the kids can color their own nutcracker ornament.

additions to the table

Bottlebrush trees are a festive and inexpensive way to bring some cheer to the table. They are easy to source and easy to paint, allowing possibilities for several different designs over the years.

As a special take-home gift for each guest, I painted these small canvases in coordinating colors for the table. Each guest also gets to take home their own ornament, placed near their drinking glass. The tabletop is a great place for party favors, and you could easily substitute small wrapped boxes, cards, or Christmas ornaments in place of the canvases for guests to enjoy long after they go home.

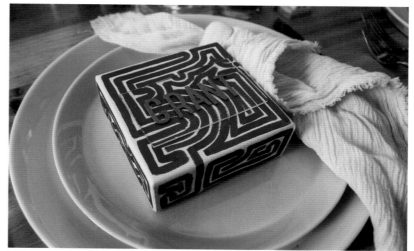

christmas variations

Like Thanksgiving, there are many ways you can get creative with reusable items each year to decorate your holiday table. You don't even always need to use Christmas-themed items—through a combination of accents, anything can take on the holiday spirit.

The texture of this decor allows for a more simple and minimalist color palette, though the multiple layers and trinkets keep it warm and fun.

White plates and white decor can work as the background for all the other pieces. Here color is added on the plate, with the drinking glasses, and with small trees throughout the center to create a warm and festive display.

Name cards don't always have to be just that. I collected vintage Scrabble tiles and arranged them on each place setting for this setup—fun and reusable, again and again.

Ornaments are the perfect way to add some character to the table, while also allowing for a little take-home memory for your guests and family.

Gift tags are an easy find during the holidays and are a quick addition to your place setting. Add some ornaments from the trees and some vintage napkins, and you can create an original tablescape without breaking the bank.

medieval rustic feast

When reading a historical book or watching a medieval movie, is there anything that looks more fun and comfortable to do with friends than a large feast? Tell me you wouldn't want to sit down with your favorite characters to enjoy a carafe of wine from a brass goblet. This table is inspired by that kind of family-style dining, with an elevated presentation. Three courses of meat? Sure, but let's do it with a floral napkin. Using fresh vegetables and fruit is a great way to bring some color to the dull, cold season. Plus, grapes are a super-refreshing chaser to a heavy bite. In the winter, we lose the sun earlier in the day, leaving us with a dark and moody evening that invites a long night gathered around the table sharing our favorite foods and favorite stories.

— MENU —

Appetizers

VEGGIE CRUDITÉS WITH ASSORTED DIPPING SAUCES, WARMED OLIVES AND NUTS

Main Dishes

KALE AND CHARD SALAD, SMOKED SAUSAGE, ROASTED CHICKEN, ROASTED MIXED VEGETABLES

Wine Pairing

SPANISH RED, ARGENTINE MALBEC, GRÜNER VELTLINER, OR OAKED CHARDONNAY

Cocktail

RASPBERRY RUM PUNCH*

Dessert

CINNAMON-POACHED PEARS*

***RECIPES FOLLOW**

cinnamon-poached pears

After a heavy, meat-filled feast, these light and sweet pears are the perfect palate cleanser.

SERVES 6

4½ cups water

6 chai tea bags

1 cup honey

6 ripe Bosc pears, peeled and cored from the bottom

1½ cups heavy cream

1 tablespoon sugar

½ tablespoon cinnamon

Bring the water to a boil in a saucepan. Remove from heat, and steep the tea bags for 8 minutes.

Remove the tea bags and stir in the honey. Add the pears and enough water to cover the pears, and bring to a simmer. Cook for 18 to 28 minutes, or until the pears are tender. Remove the pears with a slotted spoon and set aside. Bring the liquid to a boil and let it boil until syrupy, about 20 to 30 minutes. Remove from heat.

Pour the heavy cream into a mixing bowl and add the sugar and cinnamon. Whisk until the cream forms stiff peaks.

To serve, place each pear on a plate, spoon some of the packing syrup over the pear, and add a dollop of cinnamon whipped cream on the side.

raspberry rum punch

This is my all-time favorite punch that is not only tasty, but looks beautiful in the glass.

SERVES 12

4 lemons, peeled and sliced, peels reserved

⅓ cup sugar

2 cups fresh raspberries, divided

3 cups sloe gin

2 cups fresh lemon juice

1½ cups dark Jamaican rum

6 cups ice

1 ice block

2 cups chilled champagne

If you really love to mix and serve punch, the addition of a punch bowl and small glasses would be a good move for your collection.

Place the lemon peels and sugar in a large bowl and muddle to infuse. Add 1¼ cups raspberries and muddle to blend. Pour in the sloe gin, lemon juice, and rum. Add 6 cups of ice. Refrigerate the punch for at least 20 minutes.

To serve, place the ice block in the bowl and add the champagne. Garnish with lemon slices and the remaining raspberries.

Table Design Notes

When you are serving food family-style, be careful not to include too many candles or decor on the table, as it makes it difficult to dish up your dinner. For this setting, I opted for one tall candelabra at the end of the table and placed other candles off the table. You don't need to sacrifice ambiance for service if you can spread the warm candlelight elsewhere in the room.

When cutting fruit for decor, slice it to fit the direction you want it to face. So, if you want it flat on the plate, simply cut in half. Want it to be 3-D coming out from the plate? Cut it at an angle so there is a flat bottom but the top still points upward. For citrus, cut some off both ends so the flesh can face up without rolling to one side or the other.

additions to the table

This dinner party utilizes

- Wooden dinner plates
- Wooden salad plates
- Black flatware
- Red wine glasses

To bring that medieval charm, I use assorted brass goblets (thrifted over time) to serve as the water glasses on this table, so that even the nondrinkers can be transported back in time.

The dark floral napkin is a thicker toile material, so it simply needed to be measured and cut, with no seam needed to finish the edges. While they look formal, due to the design, they're a very simple and quick addition to bring the drama. Tied in a knot, they perfectly frame the pear name card.

For name cards, I use my trusty acrylic panels, snuggled into a half slice of pear.

Using veggies and fruit on the table allows for very little waste, as the uncut vegetables can be cooked later in the week and the cut vegetables can washed and used again (or, if too on edge, shared with the pup!). And all can be composted.

cozy winter brunch

One of the greatest things about living in Colorado is the active mountain lifestyle available to readily participate in. Hiking, biking, skiing, fishing, rafting . . . lots of "ings," most of which require an early-morning start. Brunch is the perfect cure to bring you back to the social world after a morning on the mountain. My parents live in Summit County, and we like to take weekend trips up with our family and friends to enjoy all that the mountains have to offer by simply opening the front door—then all coming back together to share a big meal to fuel the rest of the active day. Much of the prep can be done the night before too, so you don't have to miss out on your own mountain adventure . . . or a few extra hours of sleep.

--- MENU ---

Appetizers

FRUIT CONES*, COFFEE

Main Dishes

MIXED GREENS WITH MUSTARD VINAIGRETTE, SCRAMBLED EGGS WITH ONIONS AND MUSHROOMS, BACON AND PORK SAUSAGE, BELGIAN WAFFLES WITH FRESH FRUIT TOPPINGS

Cocktail

PEACH BELLINI*

Drinks

FRENCH-PRESS COFFEE, ESPRESSO AND FIXINGS FOR LATTES, AMERICANOS, CAPPUCCINOS

*RECIPES FOLLOW

fruit cones

A quick and easy way to serve up some sweetness.

SERVES 8

8 cups mixed berries

8 cups chopped strawberries

8 cups chopped peaches

8 waffle cones

Heavy cream

Clean and prep all the fruits and berries. Whisk the heavy cream in a bowl until stiff peaks form. To serve, add a dollop of whipped cream into the bottoms of the cones and fill each cone with a mixture of fruit.

Brunch, the meal that combines breakfast and lunch, is usually eaten between 10 a.m. and 2 p.m. and typically includes an alcoholic drink. Originating in England in the late 1800s, it became popular in the 1930s in the United States and has certainly seen a resurgence with the millennial generation. It is a meal that allows for a full Saturday of activities without worrying about waking up early, and it's a great opportunity to meet up with friends to kick-start your week.

peach bellini

This classic drink is sure to be an instant favorite and a new staple for brunch and beyond.

YIELDS 1 DRINK

1 ounce fresh peach puree

½ tablespoon freshly squeezed lemon juice

¼ teaspoon honey

6 ounces chilled prosecco

Peach slice

Add peach puree, lemon juice and honey and blend until smooth. Fill a champagne flute one-quarter full with the puree blend and top with prosecco. Garnish with a peach slice. For a mocktail version, simply substitute San Pellegrino for the prosecco! To make your own puree, blend one peach with ½ cup of water per cocktail.

Bellinis can be served in any style of stemmed glass, but I chose to go with some champagne flutes for that extra fancy feeling . . . in your pajamas.

This dinner party utilizes:

- White salad plates
- Vintage brass flatware
- Water glasses

Table Design Notes

I wanted to pack as many guests as possible in the center of the action, the kitchen. This meant opting for a tight place setting, with salad plates as the serving plates and a small centerpiece. When entertaining in close quarters, pick functional pieces that can also serve as decor for the table, like a pair of recycled glasses for water and juice.

additions to the table

Petite juice glasses are a great addition to your collection. You can use them for juice, cocktails, or even flower buds. I found a set of eight at the thrift store for two dollars.

This brunch table setting includes two napkin sets: one vintage set of cocktail/appetizer napkins with bold colors to match the berries in the fruit cones, and one neutral set to keep the table setting fresh and neat. The neutral napkin is a cotton-linen blend with a simple stitch on the end for finishing—a quick DIY and you have a versatile set of napkins for your collection.

I created edible "place cards" by using alphabet cookie cutters to cut everyone's name out of melon pieces. This is a fun addition to the table, without taking up any additional space.

I found these mini mugs and knew they would make a great addition to a brunch party. Everyone can have their own little espresso zinger to end the big meal. I think these are actually from a vintage play tea set. But if they are ceramic, they are good to go for hot beverages!

après ski party

After a morning on the mountain, or any cold outing, I just want to be teleported down to New Orleans to load up on savory, soupy, spicy filling dishes. This party is inspired by that craving and the relaxed lounging that happens up at my parents' mountain house all winter long.

Set a couple dishes to simmer on the stove while you set up little stations for food service, drink service, and seating in front of the fireplace. Feel free to change into your sweats or pajamas and put on your favorite movies, before later jumping into the hot tub for a relaxing soak!

MENU

Appetizers
ASSORTED PICKLES, OLIVES, AND FINGER FOODS, CRUDITÉS AND DIP

Main Dishes
JAMBALAYA*, GUMBO, BOUDIN BALLS

Wine Pairing
LIGHT WHITE WINE (GRÜNER VELTLINER, ALBARIÑO, PINOT GRIS)

Cocktail
BLOODY MARY BAR*

Dessert
BEIGNETS

*RECIPES FOLLOW

jambalaya

This meal is not only filling but also packed with meat and veggies, making it a healthy choice as well.

SERVES 8

½ cup extra-virgin olive oil, divided

1½ pounds boneless, skinless chicken thighs, cut into bite-size pieces

1½ pounds andouille sausage, cut into half-inch pieces

3 jalapeños, stemmed, seeded, and finely chopped

2 medium onions, finely chopped

6 cloves garlic

2 14-ounce cans crushed tomatoes

4 cups homemade or low-sodium chicken stock

2 cups long-grain rice

½ tablespoon Cajun seasoning

½ teaspoon cayenne pepper

1 bay leaf

1 pound raw large shrimp, peeled and deveined

1½ cups okra, frozen or fresh

Kosher salt and freshly cracked black pepper

Fresh parsley, chopped

Heat 2 tablespoons of the oil in a stockpot over medium-high heat. Add the chicken and sausage and sauté for 5 to 7 minutes until the meat is lightly browned and cooked through. Remove the meat from the pot and set aside.

Add the remaining oil to the pot and add the jalapeños, onions, and garlic. Sauté until the onions are softened.

Add the crushed tomatoes, chicken stock, rice, Cajun seasoning, cayenne, and bay leaf, and stir to combine. Simmer for 25 to 30 minutes until the rice is nearly cooked through, stirring occasionally to keep the rice from sticking to the bottom.

Add the shrimp and okra and continue to simmer until the shrimp are cooked through and pink.

Stir in the chicken and sausage and remove the bay leaf. Taste and season with salt, pepper, and additional Cajun seasoning if needed. Remove from the heat and serve warm with parsley to garnish.

bloody mary bar

The Bloody Mary is a classic drink that, once you ace the recipe, makes you pretty much unstoppable with the rest of the cocktail canon.

bloody mary mix

MAKES ONE PITCHER

5 cups organic tomato juice

⅓ cup Worcestershire sauce

1½ tablespoons horseradish

2 ounces lemon juice

1 ounce lime juice

1 ounce hot sauce, or more to taste

¼ teaspoon celery seed

½ teaspoon black pepper

¼ teaspoon smoked paprika

1 teaspoon salt

bloody mary cocktail

YIELDS 1 DRINK

1 teaspoon salt

½ teaspoon smoked paprika

Lime wedge

Ice

5 ounces Bloody Mary Mix

2 ounces vodka

¼ ounce lime juice

Garnishes

Make the Bloody Mary Mix. Combine all ingredients in a pitcher and mix together. Store refrigerated for up to one week.

Mix the salt and paprika together in a small shallow dish. Run a lime wedge around the rim of a highball or pint glass. Roll the rim in the salt-paprika mix to cover. Fill the glass with ice.

Combine the Bloody Mary mix, vodka, and lime juice in a cocktail shaker with ice. Shake until chilled and strain into the prepared glass. Garnish with your choice of snacks.

Garnishes: Pickle Spears, Small Whole Pickles, Green Olives, Celery Stalks, Lemon Wedges, Crispy Bacon Strips, Spicy Green Beans, Pickled Okra, Cooked Shrimp, Jerky Sticks, Cherry Tomatoes, Pearl Onions

To add a little excitement to the everyday Bloody Mary, I combine all the ingredients in my beverage dispenser with large pieces of chopped vegetables to steep more veggie flavor—and to look more interesting. For an extra kick, infuse the mix with jalapeños!

Table Design Notes

Set up small tables around the fireplace to create a cozy space to share your stories from the morning. Spread condiments across each table so guests can pop a squat and not leave until the bowl is empty.

The Après-ski tradition first became a custom in Norway in the late 1800s and quickly spread to homes and ski clubs alike. It typically takes place in the late afternoon into the early evening. Most skiers want to wake up early to hit to slopes, so this earlier gathering takes the place of late-night action. Red wine is traditionally the drink of choice, served with cheeses. Après ski has since morphed into a calorie refill that includes bloody marys, pitchers of beer, and calorie-heavy appetizers and finger foods. No matter how you celebrate, après ski is about gemütlichkeit, a German word from Austrian après-ski culture to describe a place full of hospitality, friendliness, and all-around good cheer.

additions to the table

To add a little pizzazz to the setup, I handprinted these napkins. See the following DIY to make your own, and start brainstorming your one-of-a-kind designs.

This dinner party utilizes:

- Assorted bowls
- Gold flatware
- Assorted coffee mugs
- Small tables
- Pillows, rugs, and throws from around the house
- Water glasses or tumblers for bloody marys
- Drink dispenser
- Assorted condiment bowls

how to make block-print napkins

This DIY is not only a solution for unique table linens but also a good craft to complete when stuck indoors during winter weather. Like dying linens, there are many different techniques to stamp and print your napkins. For this project we'll use rubber materials that allow for easy washing and reuse, but there are several different ways to make a stamp: potatoes, foam, wood, and other found items. Feel free to explore and experiment.

YOU WILL NEED:

- Pen
- Rubber block
- Rubber carving tool
- 1 package of finished white cotton napkins, or unfinished cotton fabric sized to a napkin
- Flattened cardboard box
- Fabric paint
- Foam roller brush or other paintbrushes
- Drying rack or ladder to dry linens on

1. **Make your stamp.** Sketch your design with a pen directly onto the rubber block. Use the carving tool to slowly carve around your design. Trim the rubber to the desired stamp size and rinse to remove any crumbs or ink from the stamp.

2. **Prepare the fabric for stamping.** Throw all the napkins or fabric into the washing machine and dryer to remove any finishes applied commercially. Once dry, lay flat on the cardboard box.

3. **Prepare the stamp.** Apply fabric paint directly to the rubber stamp with the foam roller brush or other paintbrush. Then press the stamp flat on the fabric. The cardboard underneath creates a soft landing so the fabric and stamp press together more evenly. Finish printing your design, then hang the fabric to dry.

4. **Set the dye.** Once the linens have completely dried, run them through the washing machine and dryer, or hand-wash and hang in the sun to set the dye.

Block printing is a technique that originated in East Asia to print on textiles and paper. The stamp, traditionally carved in wood, is prepared as a relief pattern in which the white areas are what is carved and cut away so the characters or patterns are inked when stamped. This traditional technique spread from China throughout the world via textile exports and religious printed texts. Today, we can recognize this technique in Indian textile designs for saris and other fashion and home fabrics designed by artisans.

PATTERN IDEAS

Shown here are finished napkins with the block print stamps. Use the images as a reference to create a similar look, or experiment on your own to create new patterns for your own block printing.

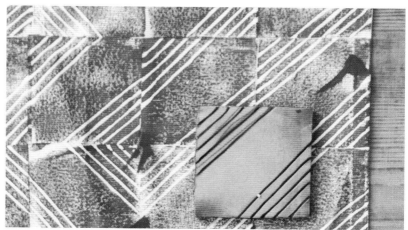

Season
spring

SPRING CAN BE ONE OF THE MOST UNPREDICTABLE seasons for weather, depending on where you live, but that should not be a reason to put off your parties for sunny summer days. This section is full of ideas for events that can go indoors or out. Rain or shine, these parties focus on shareable moments and conversation starters. Let your friendships bloom like the spring florals.

springtime garden fête

You know it is spring when the flowers start to bloom and you can sit outside for more than a few minutes because the temperature is that pleasant.

This garden-themed party can serve as a brunch, lunch, or dinner party that gets you and your favorite people outdoors.

— MENU —

Appetizers

DEVILED EGGS*, ASSORTED PICKLE PLATTER, ASPARAGUS BRUSCHETTA

Main Dishes

SPRING GREENS, GARDEN FRITTATA, POTATO SALAD, LEMON ROASTED CHICKEN

Wine Pairing

LIGHT WHITES AND ROSÉ (OR PINOT GRIGIO, PINOT GRIS, CHARDONNAY)

Cocktail

ROSÉ LEMONADE*

Dessert

ASSORTED FRESH COOKIES

*RECIPES FOLLOW

stella's deviled eggs

This secret family recipe is sure to make you a fan of this southern classic.

MAKES 24 EGGS

1 dozen large eggs

3 tablespoons sweet pickle relish, or pickles minced

¼ cup Kraft Sandwich Spread

2 tablespoons French's Classic Yellow Mustard

Kosher salt and white pepper to taste

Sliced green olives stuffed with pimento

Smoked paprika

Hard-boil the eggs and let cool. Peel the eggs and slice each in half lengthwise, dumping the yolks into a separate bowl. Place each egg half in a deviled-egg tray. Mash the yolks with a fork until finely smashed. Add the relish and sandwich spread and mix until evenly combined. Add the yellow mustard, which should thin the mixture. Add salt and pepper to taste. Fill each egg white with a teaspoon. Place an olive slice on top. Sprinkle with paprika. Refrigerate until you're ready to serve.

A staple at all of my family events is my grandmother's deviled eggs. Over the years, guests have always commented on their particular flavor standing apart and above most of the mayo/mustard deviled eggs they were used to having. My mom had always kept the secret ingredient to herself, sharing with only her closest friends and family. But we've decided these little babies are too tasty to not share with everyone! The sandwich spread adds an extra tang that will refresh this timeless appetizer for generations to come.

rosé lemonade

A super simple way to jazz up your glass of rosé.

YIELDS 1 DRINK

3 ounces rosé

1½ ounces sparkling lemonade

Lavender sprig

Pour the rosé and lemonade into a flute. Garnish with lavender.

Table Design Notes

I wanted to bring in a handmade touch to complement the spring colors and florals on the table, so I hand-drew these floral cards for each place setting. The best guides for learning to draw flowers are *How to Draw Modern Florals* and *Florals By Hand* by my friend Alli Koch. She'll help guide you to draw like a pro artist in no time.

additions to the table

I'm always on the hunt for affordable and sustainable entertaining pieces, and when I first saw these reusable bamboo flatware sets, I knew they would be the perfect complement to a minimal table and light meal.

Flowers are beautiful all on their own, no fancy centerpiece needed. I collected various glass bottles (ink wells, soda bottles, whisky bottles, medicine bottles, etc.) and lined them down the table with a single stem in each. Afterward, I tied the stems together to dry for the next time.

To pair with the bright florals on the table, I ordered this cotton fabric and folded it in a simple waterfall to nestle under each floral card.

The place cards were a quick addition with sticker letters on my standard acrylic name cards. I could also have easily written the names on the top of each floral card!

This dinner party utilizes:

- White dinner and salad plates
- Water glasses
- Wine glasses
- Bamboo flatware

shareable takeout party

I always have a hard time deciding what type of dish I want to order for takeout and usually end up ordering two to three dishes . . . per person! This takeout party is a low-key way to order the whole menu and have a little of everything. This menu features one of my favorite recipes, Thai Patty Lettuce Cups, along with all of my favorite dishes from our local Vietnamese/Chinese restaurant.

——— MENU ———

Appetizers

**EGG ROLLS, CRAB WONTONS, VIETNAMESE EGG ROLLS,
SPRING ROLLS, DUMPLINGS**

Main Dishes

**THAI PATTY LETTUCE CUPS*, BEEF LO MEIN, PORK PAD THAI,
CURRY CHICKEN, FRIED RICE, HOT WINGS**

Wine Pairing

LIGHT WHITE OR RED (SAUVIGNON BLANC, GRÜNER VELTLINER, PINOT NOIR)

Cocktail

THAI WHISKEY SOUR* AND JAPANESE BEER

Dessert

TEA AND FORTUNE COOKIES

*RECIPES FOLLOW

thai patty lettuce cups

The perfect bite of familiar and new, these sausage snacks are great as an appetizer or main dish.

MAKES 8-12 SERVINGS

8 tablespoons fish sauce, divided

½ cup oyster sauce

2 Thai chilis with seeds, minced

1 pound ground pork

1 pound ground turkey

4 shallots, minced

2 tablespoons all-purpose flour

6 garlic cloves

4 tablespoons fresh lime juice

4 tablespoons cane sugar

6 tablespoons frying oil

1 head crunchy large lettuce, leaves separated and washed

Combine 4 tablespoons of fish sauce, the oyster sauce, half of the chili and seeds, the meat, shallots, flour, and garlic in a bowl. Mix with damp hands or large spoon until evenly combined.

Shape the mixture into 2- to 3-inch patties and place on plate. Cover and chill the patties for at least 30 minutes, or overnight.

Whisk the remaining fish sauce and chilis with seeds with the lime juice, sugar, and a dash of water in a small bowl for dipping sauce.

Heat the oil in a pan over medium-high heat. Add the patties and cook until golden, 4 to 6 minutes per side. Lay each patty in a washed lettuce leaf and serve with dipping sauce.

thai whiskey sour

A whiskey sour is not what usually comes to mind for an Asian food pairing, but when you imagine the flavors of the lime juice and tamarind, bourbon is the natural choice to bring it all together.

YIELDS 1 DRINK

1½ ounces bourbon

1 ounce fresh lime juice

1 tablespoon tamarind paste diluted with 1 tablespoon water

½ ounce simple syrup

Orange slice

Luxardo maraschino cherry

Mint sprig

Fill a cocktail shaker with ice. Add the bourbon, lime juice, diluted tamarind paste, and simple syrup and shake well. Skewer the cherry and orange slice on a cocktail pick. Pour the mixture into a chilled double old-fashioned glass and garnish with the skewer and a mint sprig.

Table Design Notes

With a buffet service and no set table, be sure to clear seating areas for your guests to get comfortable. Keep napkins, soy sauce, extra chopsticks, and water pitchers in each area so guests can stay seated. If you are serving a lot of saucy foods, remove any white pillows and throw blankets and opt for other textiles that are easier to clean.

This dinner party utilizes:

- Assorted servingware
- Assorted serving bowls
- Water glasses
- Double old-fashioned glasses

additions to the table

The Chinese takeout box is uniquely American and was originally designed to hold oysters. With its waxed interior, it is nearly leakproof and perfect for any menu item—whether for this party or others to come.

These iconic takeout boxes are a great way to share dishes with guests throughout the evening and to take home at the end of the night without worrying about losing any Tupperware.

While this dinnerware is disposable, the chopsticks do not have to be. I found this vintage set at an antique mall, and it will last through many a takeout night. Just treat the chopsticks like you would other wooden pieces that are washed and tended to with care.

Like other parties, you can get festive with how you serve the food, but always have the familiar close at hand in case your guests are confused by your creativity! I assorted small plates for appetizers and salad plates with flatware on standby on the buffet table for those who are not skilled with chopsticks.

The decor is simple, with paper lanterns scattered through the house. You can use decor like this to signify the gathering areas. Paper lanterns are affordable and reusable for several occasions. Several of mine are more than fifty years old, found on eBay.

fried-everything party

When the large fryer arrived on our doorstep, everyone questioned what in the world I would be frying so often that I needed a fryer so big. The answer is: everything I can. While we only pull it out a few times a year, we certainly take advantage of the hot oil and a big batch of batter and fry up everything in the house—and never have any regrets.

This party focuses on one of my favorite foods, fried chicken. The menu works to balance the fried goodies with healthy salads and sides, while the table is set to invite getting messy, with newspaper table coverings and baking-pan dinner dishes. You have permission to chow down with friends. Then lounge around and wait for your food coma to pass.

MENU

Appetizers
FRIED OKRA, FRIED PICKLES, HUSH PUPPIES

Main Dinner
RED CABBAGE SLAW, BRUSSEL SPROUT SLAW, ASSORTED PICKLES AND ONIONS, AND FRIED CHICKEN*

Wine Pairing
SWEET WHITE (PINOT GRIGIO, MOSCATO D'ASTI, ROSÉ)

Cocktail
BEERGARITA*

Dessert
HAND PIES AND VANILLA ICE CREAM

*RECIPES FOLLOW

fried chicken

The key to my secret recipe is the overnight spent in the refrigerator. It dries the skin so it can be perfectly crunchy after its dip in the fryer.

MAKES 4 SERVINGS

3 tablespoons kosher salt

2 teaspoons paprika

1 teaspoon cayenne pepper

2 teaspoons black pepper

½ teaspoon garlic salt

1 tablespoon onion powder

8 to 10 chicken pieces

Canola or peanut oil

1 cup gluten-free pancake mix

1½ cups all-purpose gluten-free flour

3 tablespoons cornstarch

3 large eggs, beaten

Line a baking sheet with parchment paper. Mix all the spices together and slather over the chicken pieces. Place the chicken on the prepared baking sheet and keep in the refrigerator overnight.

Mix the pancake mix, flour, and cornstarch together, as well as extra spices if you wish. Dip the chicken pieces one at a time in the eggs, then coat in the flour mix.

Heat 1½ inches of oil in a large skillet. Lightly brown the chicken pieces for 4 minutes on each side. Remove and place on a baking rack over paper towels to cool slightly, then serve.

beergarita

This is a fun way to mix up the basic beer-and-chicken pairing.

YIELDS 1 DRINK

¼ cup lime juice

2 tablespoons agave syrup

1 ounce tequila

Ice

1 cup pilsner beer (such as Pacifico)

Lime wedge

In a shaker, combine the lime juice, agave, tequila, and ice. Shake well to combine, then strain into a highball or pilsner glass. Top the glass with the beer and serve garnished with a lime wedge.

This dinner party utilizes:

- Gold flatware
- Water glasses
- Assorted wooden servingware
- Assorted condiment and fruit bowls
- Pilsner or highball glasses

Table Design Notes

When serving family-style, keep all decor and lighting contained and safe for passing dishes across the table.

additions to the table

For the messiest dinners, I want to prepare as best I can for an easy cleanup. These baking pans are not only easy to clean, especially when lined with parchment paper, but with taller sides than your average dinner plate, they contain everyone's mess to their own pan.

I lined the table with newspaper to trap any grease from the family-style serving or messy hands. And it might even spark a conversation about the day's happenings!

While the vintage mason jar candles can bring that expected, down-home country feel to the table, add a few other elements to keep it exciting and unexpected, like these batik-printed rooster napkins, rattan glass holders, and two-toned pilsner glasses.

The name tag can pull double-duty as the place card and later the drink coaster as you migrate to the porch for the rest of the evening.

For spending a long evening outdoors with low-maintenance candlelight, pick up veladoras or seven-day candles, available at most grocery stores. These 8-inches-tall white candles in glass jars will last through the night, and the next night, and the next.

ladies wine tasting

As life gets more complicated it becomes harder and harder to break your routine and take a night off. Planning an organized party leaves little room for excuses, particularly when there is lots of wine to be had.

Hosting a wine tasting is a great way to chat with friends, learn about and experience some new tastes, and relax. This party is about that shared experience, and we'll explore several different ideas for how to create your perfect wine combo and feed your guests.

MENU

Appetizers
PROSECCO AND SHAREABLE CHEESE BREAD*

Main Dish
LARGE SPREAD OF CHEESE, MEAT, NUTS, AND FRUIT

Wine Pairing
ASSORTMENT OF THREE TO FIVE WINES TO TASTE**

Dessert
VANILLA GELATO TOPPED WITH A SHOT OF ESPRESSO

*RECIPE FOLLOWS
**SEE "HOW TO SELECT WINE," PAGE 167 FOR TIPS.

shareable cheese bread

There is nothing better than the pairing of bread and cheese—until you add pesto and realize what you've been missing!

MAKES 4 TO 6 SERVINGS

1 boule or round bread loaf, from the deli or homemade

1½ cups pesto

1 cup shredded havarti cheese

1 cup shredded mozzarella cheese

Olive oil for drizzling

Freshly ground pepper to taste

Preheat the oven to 400°F. Place the loaf on a baking sheet lined with parchment paper. Spoon in the pesto sauce, filling every crack in the loaf. Load all the cracks with as much cheese as possible. Drizzle olive oil over the top, then sprinkle with pepper.

Carefully tent the loaf in foil so it doesn't touch the bread. Bake for 20 minutes, then remove the foil and let the cheese brown. Watch closely so the cheese doesn't melt. Serve hot with napkins close by.

Wine-Tasting Combos

There are a few different ways you can choose which combination of wines to serve:

- **By Region:** choose a specific location and taste through several wines unique to that wine-making area.

- **By Wine Type:** choose a few different types, then sample from different regions; for example, a pinot noir from Sonoma, New Zealand, Washington State, and France.

- **Expert-Selected:** go to a time-tested wine shop and have the knowledgeable staff select the wines for you.

- **Guest-Selected:** have each guest bring their favorite wine for all to share.

Depending on the mood of the party, the serving order of the wines may not matter. However, the traditional order of service is: bubbles, light whites, rich whites, light reds, bold reds, dessert wines.

When serving food on the table that you want to encourage guests to eat, make sure it is prepared for sharing: Does it need to be cut, or is it paired with a knife? Are all of the fruits properly washed and trimmed?

I always lay wax paper underneath food that is meant to be eaten, so guests know that it is not just decoration, but meant to be touched and tasted. Plus, it means easier cleanup at the end of the night.

Table Design Notes

Similar to the grazing setup of the Moroccan (page 82), spread the different snacks across different areas of the table to avoid reaching over others.

This may seem odd—and I didn't believe it at first—but the perfect pairing and palate cleanser for this meal is a plain potato chip!

Color is an important aspect of comparing wines, so avoid colored glassware and use a solid backdrop like butcher or craft paper.

additions to the table

With the dinner spread out as the decor, it's best not to disturb the setup with decor, flowers, or candles that might confuse guests. I opted to hang flowers above the table so there is still a festive feel to the table, no one is likely to eat any petals.

I printed simple wine note cards for each guest to mark down their favorite wines or pairings. This wine party was where I confirmed that a potato chip is actually the perfect pairing for red wine—and not just a bad habit.

This dinner party utilizes:

- White salad plates
- Salad forks
- Water glasses
- Wine glasses

As a special take-home, I knotted these macramé rings for each guest. Small macramé pieces are some of my favorite table decor items because they add a bit of interest and texture to the place setting without too much color or distraction. You can learn to tie a basic macramé knot on pages 168. You'll be surprised by how much you can do with the knowledge of just a few knots.

how to select wine

Serving wine should be as simple and pleasurable as drinking it. In all my research and self-education I've learned that the best wine choice is the one that does not overwhelm you or become a burden. The simple rule of white-wine-with-white-meat and red-wine-with-red-meat works just fine, but is often too limiting and expected for a novice wine server. Instead, base your selections on one of these three concepts: sameness, contrast, or intensity.

SAMENESS

For sameness, pair wines with foods that seem to have the same or similar characteristics. For instance, rich food with rich wines, light food with light wines. Sometimes too much of the same can be boring, as it all starts to meld together, so try to match to the main dish with a contrasting side.

CONTRAST

Contrast is at the base of many of your favorite pairings—think salty cheese with a sweet wine—but sometimes this concept can actually work the two tastes against each other. Again, as with sameness, work to pair or contrast with one part of the dish while complementing with another.

INTENSITY

With intensity, pair strength of taste with strength of wine. For instance, a delicate sweet wine paired with a spicy, hearty dish will get lost in the richness of the food. But a peppery syrah or full-bodied red can both hold its own alongside such a dish and add a nice, complementary finish.

All in all, the best way to find the best wines is through your own trial and error. These days, notes on your favorites (or least favorites) can be kept within an app on your phone with a shared network of reviews and other people's notes on their favorites. Through your experiments, find your favorites to pair with your most-shared dishes and favorite flavors, including varying meats, spice levels, and textures. I have go-to picks for steak, pastas, pork, curries, grilled veggies, roasted veggies, chicken of all kinds, charcuterie trays, popcorn, leftovers . . . there is a good pairing for all of your favorites.

BASIC WINE AND CHEESE PAIRINGS

Wine	Cheese	Fruits, Veggies, or Nuts	Meat, Bread, or Crackers
chardonnay	brie	pear slices	baguette slices
merlot	gouda	dried apricots	crisp crackers
cabernet sauvignon	sharp white cheddar	red grapes	peppered salumi
chianti	parmesan	castelvetrano olives	crunchy breadsticks
sauvignon blanc	gruyère	pistachios	baguette slices
riesling	blue cheese & honey	walnuts	thick crackers
pinot grigio	ricotta	sun-dried tomatoes	thin crisps
sauvignon blanc	mozzarella	fresh tomatoes & basil strips	multi-seed crackers
malbec	sharp orange cheddar	dates	dried cherry crackers
pinot noir	manchego	cranberries & almonds	dark bread slices
shiraz	smoked gouda	figs	prosciutto
prosecco	camembert	strawberries	salted potato chips

how to tie a basic macramé knot

These two knots can get you many different designs and creations. The Reverse Larkshead is the knot that you use to secure all the rope to your anchor, while the square is the basic knot that can be used to fashion the rest of your piece.

YOU WILL NEED:

- Macramé cord
- Wooden dowel

REVERSE LARKSHEAD KNOT

- Fold one macramé cord in half, and place it loop-down beneath your anchor with the cords facing down **(A)**.

- Pull the loop up over the dowel. Pull the cords down through the loop, creating a pretzel shape **(B)**.

- Pull the two cords together to secure the knot at the top **(C)**.

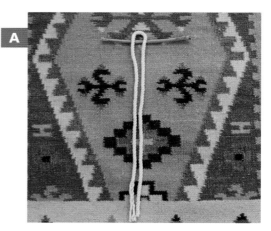

SQUARE KNOT

- Begin with two Reverse Larkshead Knots to create four working cords. The two outer cords are the knotting cords, and the two middle cords are the knot-bearing cords (**D**).

- Bring the left knotting cord to the right, over the two knot-bearing cords and underneath the right knotting cord (**E**).

- Bring the right knotting cord to the left, under the two knot-bearing cords and over the left knotting cord. Pull to secure the half knot (**F, G**).

- Bring the right knotting cord to the left, over the two knot-bearing cords and underneath the left knotting cord (**H**).

- Bring the left knotting cord to the right, under the two knot-bearing cords and over the right knotting cord. Pull to secure the square knot (**I, J**).

If you repeat the first three steps again and again, you will create a spiral pattern with your knots, a great way to add some interest to a piece without any complex knots (photos below).

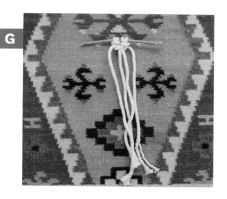

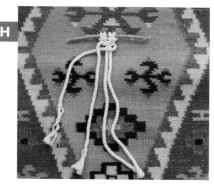

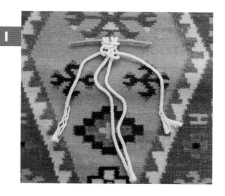

Season summer

SUNSHINE IS THE ULTIMATE REASON FOR gathering with friends outdoors, and summer is full of it. But the party ideas in this section will keep you lingering around the table long after the sun sets.

portable picnic party

There is no better way to escape your to-do list than to escape to the outdoors. Whether a park, picnic area, or your own backyard, just grab your basket and blankets and transport yourself to a low-key, laid-back gathering.

To start, try a few new and interesting jarred or canned snacks, such as fish, olives, or individually wrapped cheeses or meats. These are easy to pack and keep longer than fresh deli food. For drinks, measure your alcohol out beforehand in small jars so they are easy to mix on the spot and you have fewer large items to carry with you to your picnic location.

— MENU —

Appetizers
ASSORTED CANNED AND INDIVIDUALLY WRAPPED SNACKS

Main Dinner
WATERMELON SLICES, RED CABBAGE SLAW, ITALIAN PRESSED SANDWICHES*

Wine Pairing
LIGHT WHITE WINE, SUCH AS VINO VERDE

Cocktail
COLLINS ON THE GO*

Dessert
ASSORTED IMPORTED COOKIES

*RECIPES FOLLOW

italian pressed sandwiches

These easy-to-prep sandwiches are great for many occasions, due to their packability and versatility.

MAKES 3 TO 4 SERVINGS

1 loaf ciabatta bread or focaccia

2 tablespoons pesto

2 tablespoons extra-virgin olive oil

6 to 8 slices salami

6 to 8 slices prosciutto

1 large mozzarella ball, sliced

1 large tomato, sliced and halved

1 large bunch basil, leaves plucked from the stem

Twine and parchment paper

Slice the loaf in half. Evenly spread pesto on one half and olive oil on the other. Layer the meats on either half of the bread first, followed by the cheese, tomatoes, and basil. Set the other half of the bread on top.

Wrap parchment paper very tightly around the whole sandwich and use twine, evenly spaced at the center of each planned individual sandwich slice, to tie it together.

Refrigerate for at least 1 hour, or overnight. Remove the wrapped sandwich from the fridge and use a serrated knife to slice the loaf into individual sandwich slices about 3-inches wide each. Leave the sandwiches wrapped for easy transport and clean eating.

collins on the go

Hot days call for lemonade, and picnics call for a cocktail. This simple recipe is the answer for those warm summer picnic days.

YIELDS 1 DRINK

6 ounces lemonade

2 ounces gin

Ice

Dash of San Pellegrino

Lemon wedge

Store and transport the lemonade in a mason jar; the jar should be about half-full. Use a small mason jar to store and transport the gin.

Add the gin to lemonade jar and fill with ice. Shake for 15 seconds, until the jar is chilled. Open and top with San Pellegrino. Garnish with a lemon wedge.

Some places are finicky about alcohol in public—using inconspicuous containers is a way to keep critics at bay. For this picnic I use two sizes: a small one for the pre-measured liquor and a larger one for the mixer. Simply pour the liquor from the small jar into the larger one, mix, and enjoy.

This dinner party utilizes:

- Gold flatware
- Water glasses
- Salad plates
- Assorted condiment and fruit bowls
- Breadboards
- Picnic baskets
- Wine glasses
- Assorted small serving utensils

additions to the table

Picnic baskets are a great thrifted find that can be used in various ways around the house until that perfect day you want to pack it up with goodies and head outdoors. I have several different types and sizes that I utilize for other purposes like storing linens, toys, and glassware.

I lined one of the picnic baskets with foil and plastic to create a makeshift cooler to keep our snacks and drinks cool.

You don't always need a large blanket to serve as your picnic area. I brought several textiles to layer and create a larger space for seating, and they take up much less space in the picnic basket.

tuscan tavola

On my first trip to Italy, I immediately understood the obsession that most visitors have for the beautiful country and rich culture. We didn't have any plans or set tours—we just went to eat, see, and experience. That two-week trip changed my approach to cooking, drinking, and living. *Tavola* means "table" in Italian. This Tuscan-themed dinner party allows us to travel back to those memories with a taste of Tuscany, and now you can explore and experience it with your loved ones too—so come, join us at the table.

MENU

Appetizers

FLATBREAD COMBOS*, ITALIAN-THEMED CHEESE BOARD

Main Dishes

FRIED ZUCCHINI FLOWERS, BRAISED ARTICHOKES, PASTA WITH ZUCCHINI PESTO, STUFFED TURKEY BREAST

Wine Pairing

ITALIAN TUSCAN REDS (CHIANTI, SANGIOVESE, BARBERA, MONTEPULCIANO), PINOT GRIGIO, PROSECCO

Cocktail

SGROPPINO*

Dessert

STRAWBERRY TART WITH CREAM

*RECIPES FOLLOW

flatbread combinations

There isn't a bad combination for flatbread, but these three options are easy to make and sure to please.

mushroom, garlic, and parmesan flatbread

MAKES 3 FLATBREADS

6 teaspoons olive oil, divided

½ pound button or baby bella mushrooms, cleaned and sliced very thin

1 cup thinly sliced onion

6 cloves garlic, chopped

1 pound fresh pizza dough (homemade or from the deli)

¾ teaspoon kosher salt

1¾ cups freshly shaved parmesan cheese

fresh cracked black pepper, to taste

3 teaspoons tarragon, divided

Wax paper

Crushed red pepper

Preheat the oven to 475°F. In a skillet, heat 1 teaspoon of olive oil over medium-high heat. Add the mushrooms, onions, and garlic and sauté until soft, about 5 to 6 minutes. Salt to taste. Use a slotted spoon to remove the veggies to a paper towel–lined plate to drain.

Divide the dough into three equal-sized pieces. Roll each piece into a thick oblong shape with a rolling pin. Place the dough on wax paper on a baking sheet. Bake for 3 to 6 minutes, then flip and bake for another 3 to 6 minutes. Remove from the oven.

Turn the oven to broil. Brush each flatbread with the remaining olive oil, sprinkle with salt and evenly spread the mushroom mixture on each flatbread. Add a heavy sprinkle of parmesan across each flatbread and top each with 1 teaspoon of chopped tarragon and black pepper to taste. Place in the oven and broil until golden. Remove and serve hot. Top with crushed red paper as needed.

cheddar, pancetta, apple, and arugula flatbread

MAKES 3 FLATBREADS

1 pound fresh pizza dough (homemade or from the deli)

3 cups grated or crumbled aged white cheddar

¾ cup diced, cooked pancetta or bacon

Black pepper, to taste

1 large apple, cored and thinly sliced

3 handfuls fresh baby arugula

Preheat the oven to 475°F. Divide the dough into three equal-sized pieces. Roll each piece into a thick oblong shape with a rolling pin. Place the dough on wax paper on a baking sheet. Bake for 3 to 6 minutes, then flip and bake for another 3 to 6 minutes. Remove from the oven.

Top the breads with the cheddar and cooked pancetta. Season with black pepper to taste. Arrange the sliced apples on top. Bake in the oven for 7 to 10 minutes, or until the cheese is melted and golden and the apples have softened. Allow to cool, then top with fresh arugula.

brussels sprouts flatbread

MAKES 3 FLATBREADS

1 pound fresh pizza dough (homemade or from the deli)

1½ cups whole-milk ricotta cheese

1½ cups shredded parmesan cheese, divided

8 small cloves garlic, minced

3 teaspoons fresh lemon juice

Crushed red pepper flakes, to taste

Kosher salt and freshly ground pepper, to taste

3 tablespoons olive oil

3 cups thinly sliced brussels sprouts

¾ cups thinly sliced red onions

1½ cups shredded mozzarella cheese

Lemon wedges for serving

Preheat the oven to 475°F. Divide the dough into three equal-sized pieces. Roll each piece into a thick oblong shape with a rolling pin. Place the dough on wax paper on a baking sheet. Bake for 3 to 6 minutes, then flip and bake for another 3 to 6 minutes. Remove from the oven.

In a small bowl, stir together the ricotta cheese, ¾ cup of the parmesan cheese, minced garlic, fresh lemon juice, crushed red pepper, and salt and black pepper to taste. Set aside.

In a small skillet, heat the olive oil over medium-high heat. Add the sliced brussels sprouts and red onion. Cook for 3 to 5 minutes, or until the vegetables are softened. Set aside.

Spread the ricotta-cheese mixture over the warmed flatbreads with a spatula. Top evenly with the shredded mozzarella cheese, remaining parmesan cheese, and brussels-sprouts mixture.

Bake the flatbreads for 10 to 12 minutes, or until the cheese is melted and the flatbread is golden-brown. Remove from the oven and squeeze a little fresh lemon juice over the top. Sprinkle with extra cheese, if desired.

sgroppino

This slushy, refreshing combo is common in Italy as a palate cleanser or dessert and is the perfect way to cool off in the summer heat.

YIELDS 1 DRINK

⅓ cup lemon sorbet

3 ounces prosecco

1 ounce vodka

In a stainless steel or chilled cocktail shaker, whisk together the sorbet and a splash of prosecco until well-mixed. Slowly pour in the vodka and remaining prosecco, while continuing to whisk. Serve in a martini or coupe glass.

This dinner party utilizes:

- White dinner plates
- Wooden salad plates
- Wooden flatware
- Water glasses
- Wine glasses
- Cake stands

Table Design Notes

Sometimes the most beautiful decor comes straight off the tree. I layered fruit from my yard, my neighbors' yards, and the grocery store to bring the season's best colors centerstage. Using assorted baskets and cake stands, you can layer the fruits to make a perfect still life scene.

additions to the table

When we were in Venice, I really wanted to bring home a lace tablecloth to enjoy at home, but I couldn't justify the cost. So instead, I looked up common Italian lace designs online and stayed on the hunt in my local antique shops and online until I found one in my budget.

For florals, I bought a few fresh greens from the grocery store, then foraged through the alleyway for all the pretty weeds. Simply add to a pretty pitcher and place among the fruit.

I wanted the beauty of the fruit to stand as the focal point, so I paired the decor with handmade linen napkins in a neutral color and sandy tiles for texture.

how to build the perfect cheese board

Cheese boards are the perfect complementary appetizer for any meal or gathering. Whether you have twenty guests or one, there is something for everyone. Charcuterie trays are my husband's love language. I'll often prep a small plate on a cutting board, or whatever is easily available, with a random bottle of wine from the discount rack at our local wine shop to greet him after a long day of crunching numbers at work. Even on a weathered cutting board or right out of the containers, a cheese board is a great way to shift the day back to what is important through easy conversation and lots of tasty bites.

COLLECTION PIECES NEEDED:

- Large board or collection of boards
- Fruit bowls
- Small condiment bowls
- Condiment spoons
- Condiment spreader
- Cheese knives

Cheese Knife Guide

Spatula knife: ideal for soft-ripened cheeses like brie and camembert, or for breaking chips off firm cheeses like asiago, romano, and parmesan.

Plane knife: use to cut semi-firm cheeses like cheddar, provolone, and gouda.

Cheese fork: use to hold a block of cheese while you slice with a knife, or to break aged cheese into crumbles.

Coure knife: use to score the rind of hard cheese, open wheels, divide wedges, and cut cheese into bite-sized pieces.

BUILD YOUR BOARD STEP-BY-STEP

1. **Pick the Board:** Consider the size, material, and number of hands grabbing items, with the idea of ease of sharing as the first and foremost goal.

2. **Choose the Cheese:** You want a good mix of textures, strengths, colors, and shapes so everyone can get a full range of tastes and experiment with different combinations. Lean more on mild, familiar cheeses and go small with the more poignant and strong varieties.

3. **Add Something Salty:** Whether hard or soft, salt pairs perfectly with all cheese varieties. Layer in cured meats, olives, and roasted and salted nuts. Consider the main meal when deciding what pairings you'd prefer. Serving a heavy meat dish? Pare down the charcuterie and add more olives and nuts.

CHEESE

SALT

SWEET

4. **Add Something Sweet:** Now a little chaser for the strong flavors from the cheese and salty sides. Dried and fresh fruit, such as sun-dried tomatoes, and snacky vegetables are great options.

5. **Time for Crunch:** Here you can play favorites and include less variety, but always go for high quantity, as everyone wants a little crunch to pair with their favorite cheese. Combine a mix of crackers, breads, bread slices, and breadsticks on your board.

6. **Don't Forget Dips:** Whether for the cheese or crackers or all on their own, little bottles and spoons can lend a special treat for all pairings. Include honey, fancy mustards, spreads, jams, and preserves.

7. **Fill in the Gaps:** Remember that everything on the board will be inviting for eating, so fill in empty spaces with garnishes that, if not in flavor, at least aromatically complement the pairings. Rosemary, thyme, basil, and other herbs are a tasty and decorative option.

CRUNCH

DIPS

GARNISH

summer bbq bash

Summer, to me, is juicy melon bites and spicy barbecue sauce before a jump in the pool. I grew up in Texas, where barbecue is a religion—and like church, you pay your respects once a week. My grandparents have a blue-tiled pool with a wooden deck and large tree for shade where they hosted parties and get-togethers every week. We lived in our swimsuits and sunnies.

   Now, living away from Texas and those pool-filled summers, barbecue is my way to have a taste of nostalgia. This menu is a mix of old and new, paying respect to my traditional Texas-BBQ past and plant-based, foodie-centric present.

MENU

Appetizers

ASSORTED PICKLES AND OLIVES, MELON-BALL SKEWERS, CUCUMBER SALAD, SAUTÉED SHISHITO PEPPERS

Main Dishes

COLESLAW, PESTO-GRILLED CORN*, CHILLED MACARONI SALAD, TATER TOTS, PORK RIBS AND BEEF BRISKET, TEXAS TOAST

Wine Pairing

SWEET WHITE (PINOT GRIGIO, MOSCATO D'ASTI)

Cocktail

BEERGRONI*

Dessert

PEACH COBBLER AND VANILLA ICE CREAM

*RECIPES FOLLOW

pesto-grilled corn

A classic BBQ pairing with a tasty twist.

MAKES 8 SERVINGS

corn

8 ears corn, husked

2 tablespoons olive oil

1 cup pesto

½ cup grated pecorino

pesto

3 cups loosely packed basil

2 large cloves garlic

¼ cup toasted pine nuts

¼ cup grated parmesan cheese

2 teaspoons lemon juice

½ cup olive oil

¼ teaspoon black pepper

Make the pesto. In a blender or food processor, combine the basil, garlic, and pine nuts. Pulse until finely chopped. Add the cheese and lemon juice and pulse again. With the motor running, drizzle in the olive oil until the pesto reaches the desired consistency. Season with black pepper.

Grill the corn. Preheat the grill to high. Brush the corn with olive oil and grill until slightly charred, 8 to 10 minutes, turning occasionally.

Brush the grilled corn with pesto and sprinkle with grated pecorino.

beergroni

With a dash of Campari, turn an ordinary barbecue beer into a memorable cocktail.

YIELDS 1 DRINK

½ ounce Campari

½ ounce gin

1 tablespoon vermouth

2 tablespoons orange juice

1 cup lager beer (such as Peroni)

Orange peel

In a cocktail shaker filled with ice, combine Campari, gin, vermouth, and orange juice. Shake well and strain into a highball or pilsner glass. Top with the beer and serve garnished with orange peel.

This dinner
party utilizes:

- Water glasses
- Wooden flatware
- Baking tins
- Beverage bucket

Table Design Notes

Keeping the table decor simple with old kombucha bottles and wildflowers off the mountain, makes it easy to set up decorative items while you labor over the slow-cooked meats.

additions to the table

Like the Fried-Everything Party (page 152), this meal might get a little messy, and as you're migrating from the buffet table to the long table in the trees, you want to make sure everything stays on your plate—so bring on the baking pans.

I accumulated quite the set of kombucha bottles over a few months that I regularly utilize as bulb or stem vases. For this party, I filled them with wildflowers gathered from around my parents' house.

Invite guests to bring their favorite six-pack to share with the group. Have a large bucket of ice waiting, and distribute the beers as everyone is finding their seats.

I found this set of small cast-iron dishes and knew they would be the perfect detail to set this dinner apart, especially when filled with homemade cornbread.

These dual-purpose name cards and coasters are great for guests to keep with them as they migrate through the night with their beer or drink.

No traditional tablecloth is needed. I laid out my collection of indigo textiles down the table to hide any sauce stains and keep beer rings off the table. Neutral, handmade luncheon-sized napkins keep the focus on the outdoors.

bohemian backyard blowout

This is the ultimate bohemian dinner party: floor seating, pillow-filled lounges, super colorful, florals, candles, wicker, layered rugs, and tasty snack foods meant to share.

This party idea not exclusive to summer and can be used for a multitude of celebrations, from birthdays to weddings. Whenever you want to get cozy and relax in a magical setting, whip out a little of everything and invite over your favorite people.

MENU

Appetizers
CHAPATI, BAKED PAKORA*, AND DIPPING SAUCES: MINT CHUTNEY, TOMATO CHUTNEY, YOGURT

Main Dishes
CHANA MASALA, CHICKEN CURRY, TANDOORI SKEWERS, BASMATI RICE, ONION-TOMATO SALAD, SAAG ALOO

Wine Pairing
FLAVORFUL REDS (MALBEC, PINOT NOIR, MERLOT)

Cocktail
JAL JEERA MOJITO*

Dessert
RAW MANGO AND PINEAPPLE SKEWERS

*RECIPES FOLLOW

baked pakora

The perfect appetizer for all diets, these crunchy veggie bites are sure to be gone quick.

MAKES 8 SERVINGS

3 large carrots

3 small potatoes

3-inch piece of ginger

1½ teaspoons kosher salt

3 teaspoons onion powder

Freshly ground black pepper, to taste

1½ teaspoons cumin seeds

3 teaspoons curry powder or garam masala

3 handfuls parsley, chopped

2½ cups garbanzo flour

Preheat the oven to 480°F. Line a baking tray with parchment paper. Grate the carrots and potatoes, leaving the skins on. Grate the ginger and combine in a large bowl with the carrots and potatoes, spices, parsley, and garbanzo flour.

Mix thoroughly with your hands until combined. Spoon 1- to 2-inch dollops on the prepared baking tray. Bake for 25 to 30 minutes. Enjoy with chutney, mint pesto, or yogurt.

jal jeera mojito

This spicy take on a mojito is sure to complement all palates.

YIELDS 1 DRINK

Sprig of mint leaves, stems removed

Lime wedge

1 teaspoon Jal Jeera masala spice mix

3 ounces club soda

½ teaspoon lime juice

½ teaspoon tamarind paste, diluted with ½ teaspoon water

1½ ounces vodka

Ice

Muddle the mint leaves and lime wedge in a highball glass. Add the Jal Jeera spice mix, then pour club soda into the glass. Stir until the spices dissolve. Add the lime juice, tamarind paste, vodka, and ice. Garnish with a mint sprig.

This dinner party utilizes:

- White dinner plates
- Gold flatware
- Colored goblets
- Wine glasses

Table Design Notes

Unless you make your own, low tables are not a common find. I fashion them in many different ways using lots of different pairings. They all have their unique purpose, but the best option is a tabletop, door, or piece of plywood set on top of a study box or boxes. You want to be able to nestle your feet under the table to be comfortable for a longer period of time.

I made these tables by placing my folding tables on top of canvas cots.

Since the table is low, keep the centerpiece low as well so guests can look across the table at one another. I combined votive candles with flowerheads in various colors and floral varieties.

additions to the table

Large lanterns are a great addition to your collection that can hang out most of the year on the patio and be pulled into the scene for outdoor gatherings.

The start of a summer night can still hold the heat of the day, so consider collecting rattan or other reusable fans to share with guests at warm gatherings.

I gathered pillows and rugs from around the house to pile on the canvas cots to create lounge areas inside the yurt for a fun way to spend the rest of the evening after clearing the table.

I lined candle votives in assorted colors along the center of the table. I have five different sets, but the key to mixing and matching is to choose a similar color story or style when building your collection. Tealights burn down quickly, so either opt for refillable oil jars or keep a handful of candles close by for refills.

These hand dishes were intended as catchalls, but I loved the idea of using them on a table to cradle blooms and nestle between candles.

resources *and* post-party tips

cleaning up post-party

Cleanup is the least fun part of any party or gathering. But with the tips below, you can minimize the work required after the last guest leaves.

- **Avoid as many dishes as possible.** Whether in prepping the food or the table, try to avoid using more than you need. For most oven-prepared foods, I use a sheet of wax paper between the food and the pan, so I can easily throw out the paper and rinse the dish quickly.

- **Set out a few more zones for dirty dishes and trash.** If there is a big pile of dirty dishes near the sink, you won't have room to get to work. Create a separate area designated for dirty dishes that is within reach of the sink, but not crowding it.

- **Plan for pre-party cleaning.** When setting up your timeline, make sure you have time to run a load in the dishwasher or hand-wash all of the prep dishes and put them away so the dishwasher and sink are empty and ready for filling post-party.

- **Keep it under control so you can have fun.** If you are someone who is really bothered by dishes in the sink, make sure you are prepared to slip them into the dishwasher, or have the sink filled with soapy water with the dish rack sitting out so you can quickly scrub and set to dry. If you don't mind the dishes sitting until morning, then don't worry about it and enjoy the night.

- **Try mass bucket cleaning.** Sometimes a big party could take several loads—and days—in the dishwasher to recover from. To save on time and water, I use this bucket trick out on the patio or driveway. Load all the dishes into a leak-proof, waterproof bucket. Top with dish soap, then spray down with the garden hose. Let the dishes sit for a few hours, empty the water into the yard, then carry indoors to rinse, dry, and put away.

cleaning vintage or thrifted finds for use

Vintage or thrift stores are amazing resources for unique, sustainable pieces you can add to your entertaining collection. But just like vintage clothes need to be handled a certain way before use, so do vintage home items.

Most dishware items can be hand-washed or machine-washed, just like their new counterparts. When in doubt, hand-wash for the first cleaning. Wooden servingware or dishware should be hand-washed, then soaked in a vinegar soak/wash, then treated with food-safe mineral oil.

- **The biggest issue with thrifted goods is typically the sale stickers, which might have been on the item for several years.** Below are some tried and true ways to remove those terrible stickers.

- **Hot water and paper towel:** Hold a folded paper towel under piping-hot water, then press on the sticker for a good minute or two. Slowly peel back the sticker and apply the paper towel again in sections reluctant to come up. Wipe a few times for the stubborn leftovers to roll up and off.

- **Razor blade:** Very delicately use the razor blade to get under the sticker as you slowly peel it off.

- **Hairdryer:** Similar to the paper-towel method, heat up the sticker, then slowly peel off the tag.

For some thrifted, or even garage sale finds, the price is marked directly on the product with a marker or crayon. You can use a magic eraser for most types of markings, and Goof Off for paint markers.

Linens, if not dry-clean only, should go straight into the washing machine on hot (if it will not damage the fabric), adding a tablespoon of borax and a half cup of white vinegar to the load. Dry on hot or lay out in the hot sun to dry.

taking care of your collection

CARING FOR WOODEN PIECES

Consistent washing, detergents, and differing climates draw oil from your wood pieces, causing them to lose their luster, become faded, and even crack. Scrub with hot, soapy water after each use, but do not soak the pieces or the wood may crack or warp.

To keep your wooden pieces in top condition, oil them regularly. You will learn how often your pieces need to be oiled based on use and your home climate. You need very few supplies to keep your wood looking healthy: a soft cloth or paper towel, mineral oil, or other food-safe oil.

To oil, start with a clean piece that has been well-scrubbed and is thoroughly dry. Using a cloth or paper towel, apply the oil liberally in an even layer over the wood. Allow the oil to soak in, overnight if possible. If the wood feels oily or sticky, buff any remaining residue away with a clean, dry cloth or paper towel.

CARING FOR ANTIQUE SILVER

Avoid contact with household chemicals, rubber, chlorinated water, or any substances that contain sulfur (e.g., mayonnaise, eggs, mustard, onions, latex, wool), as they will cause corrosion and tarnish. Direct sunlight also causes silver to tarnish, so keep your pieces tucked away in a cabinet or closet.

Simply polishing your silver works well when the tarnishing is not too severe. Silver is soft and can become scratched easily, so you must use a special silver cloth, lint-free flannel, microfiber, or other soft, nonabrasive cloth. Do not use paper towels or tissues to polish your pieces, as they contain fibers that can scratch the silver. Use long back-and-forth motions that mirror the grain of the silver. Rubbing in circles will magnify any tiny scratches. Use a cotton swab to get into small, detailed areas. Excessive polishing can remove the plating on silver-plated items, so do so sparingly.

When the polishing cloth isn't enough to remove tarnish, you can make your own environmentally friendly silver cleaner using ingredients from your kitchen.

- **Soap and water:** Warm water and organic dishwashing soap should be the first line of defense if the polishing cloth fails. This should also be used before any other cleaner is applied.

- **Baking soda and water:** Create a paste of baking soda and water and use a clean cloth to apply a pea-sized amount to the silver and polish. For detailed items, thin the paste with water and use a clean toothbrush to get the cracks and crevices. Rinse the piece under running warm water, and dry with a clean cloth.

- **Olive oil and lemon juice:** Mix ½ cup lemon juice with 1 tsp. olive oil in a bowl. Dip a small cloth in the solution and wring it out so that it doesn't drip, then polish the silver, rinse, and dry.

- **White vinegar and baking soda:** Use this solution to remove heavy tarnish that's preventing you from polishing your silver. Soak the tarnished piece in a solution of ½ cup white vinegar and 2 tbsp. baking soda for two to three hours, then rinse and dry.

CARING FOR ANTIQUE BRASS

While the tarnish of some brass pieces can bring a lot of character, those used with food should be kept clean and free of too much patina. There are many commercial brass polishes that work well, including: Brasso, Bar Keepers Friend, and Wright's Brass Polish.

For an organic cleaner, you can make a combination similar to the homemade silver-care recipes.

- **Lemon juice and baking soda:** Combine the juice of half a lemon with 1 tsp. of baking soda and stir until it becomes a paste. Apply the paste with a soft cloth to your piece. If the tarnish is heavy, let the piece sit with the paste on it for thirty minutes, then rinse and dry. Repeat multiple times if necessary.

- **Lemon and salt:** Slice a lemon in half and cover the cut section with a teaspoon of table salt. Rub the lemon on the piece, squeezing it as you go to release the juice, then rinse and dry.

CARING FOR LINENS

Most specialty linens can be machine-washed on a gentle cycle. Cotton napkins can be washed the same way you wash your cotton clothes. Shake linens warm from the dryer and loosely fold for storage. If needed, napkins can be ironed before use—plan for that chore in your timeline. Store vintage napkins and tablecloths wrapped around a large tube, like that which comes from a large bolt of fabric or a PVC pipe remnant, rather than folded, to avoid creases that can weaken the fibers over time.

where to shop for your tabletop

There are some wonderful small boutique shops out there selling beautiful wares, but for the purpose of this list, I want to share those that are the most available to the most people.

BASIC PIECES TO BUILD YOUR COLLECTION

- Crate and Barrel
- CB2
- Williams-Sonoma
- Sur La Table
- Food52

SPECIALTY PIECES, DRINKWARE, OR SERVINGWARE

- Anthropologie
- World Market
- T.J. Maxx, HomeGoods, Marshalls
- eBay
- Etsy
- ShopGoodwill (shopgoodwill.com)
- Swahili Modern (swahilimodern.com)
- Elsie Green (elsiegreen.com)
- Suite One Studio
- Hygge Life
- Fleastyle
- Online vintage vendors, such as Simplychi Vintage, Indigo Trade, Meek Vintage, etc.
- Local thrift stores
- Local antique stores

finding inspiration for your event

Yes, you can get lost on social media drooling over dinner parties . . . or, you can let your favorite things be the inspiration you need to throw an event. A good recipe, a random thrift find, or no reason at all except that you want to be around your favorite people—these are all good reasons to host an event.

The key is to channel the vibe you want to create into the party. Your effort should match the comfort level you want your guests to feel. Make the focus of the night be on one another, not the social-media opportunities. Large budgets and overdecorating can often distract from the heart of the matter—gathering and celebrating with friends.

FURTHER READING ON BOHEMIAN-INSPIRED DESIGN

The New Bohemians, by Justina Blakeney

The New Bohemians Handbook, by Justina Blakeney

The Maverick Soul, by Miv Watts

Urban Jungle, by Igor Josifovic and Judith de Graaff

Surf Shack, by Nina Freudenberger

Habitat, by Lauren Liess

Get It Together!, by Orlando Soria

FURTHER READING ON ENTERTAINING AND COOKING

3-Ingredient Cocktails, by Robert Simonson

Apertif, by Rebekah Peppler

Tiki, by Shannon Mustipher

Platters and Boards, by Shelly Westerhausen

First We Eat, by Eva Kosmas Flores

Decorate for a Party, by Holly Becker and Leslie Shewring

The Flower·Recipe Book, by Alethea Harampolis and Jill Rizzo

Simple Gatherings, by Melissa Michaels

YOUR EVERYDAY COLLECTION

White dinner plates, white salad plates, white fruit/cereal bowls, wooden dinner plates, wooden salad plates, red wine

Glasses: Crate & Barrel
Gold flatware: Target
Wooden bowls: vintage
Smoke juice glasses: vintage
Biergarten folding tables: Amazon.com

HARVEST PARTY

Wooden taper candle holders: vintage, Target
Terra-cotta chargers: Home Depot (or any garden store)
Green wine glasses: Tuesday Morning
Rattan cup holders: vintage (assorted thrift stores)
Recycled juice glasses: vintage, Target
Name-card tiles: Goodwill
Olive oil bottles: Tuesday Morning
Wine Carrier: wholesale purchase for hunt & gather
Plain white napkins for dying: Amazon.com
Acrylic place cards: handmade
Olive oil dipping bowls: vintage (eBay)
Highball glasses: Crate & Barrel
Rattan bar placemats: vintage (estate sale)
Spritz goblets: vintage (family pieces)
Bar tools: vintage (thrift store)

TACO BAR PARTY

Wooden flatware: Target
Assorted cacti: IKEA, Whole Foods, local garden store
Napkins: vintage (flea markets)
Milagros: antique mall, eBay
Paper picado banners: Amazon.com
Buffet table tablecloth: vintage (flea market)
Moscow mule mugs: T.J. Maxx, Marshalls
Toppings bowls: West Elm
Terracotta serving dishes: wholesale purchase for hunt & gather
Rattan pitcher: vintage (thrift store)

MOROCCAN TAPAS PARTY

Moroccan side plates: wholesale purchase for hunt & gather
Assorted dipping bowls: assorted travel locations, Anthropologie, wholesale purchase for hunt & gather

Wooden boards: T.J. Maxx, thrift stores, flea markets, wholesale purchase for hunt & gather
White cake stands: Marshalls
Aluminum bowls: wholesale purchase for hunt & gather
Recyclable bamboo flatware: Anthropologie
Rattan side tables: IKEA, thrift stores, flea markets, Craigslist
Army cots: Craigslist, flea markets
Assorted pillows: wholesale purchase for hunt & gather, World Market, Target
Moroccan pom-pom blanket: wholesale purchase for hunt & gather
Moroccan tray table: wholesale purchase for hunt & gather
Moroccan lanterns: Target, Amazon.com
Gold Moroccan highballs glasses: T.J. Maxx
Assorted baskets: thrift stores, antique malls
Small serving forks: Sur La Table
Small Moroccan tagines: wholesale purchase for hunt & gather
Persian rug: eBay
Paper straws: King Soopers
Tea pitcher: thrift store
Rattan serving trays: vintage (garage sales)
Large rattan chair: estate sale
Napkins: handmade

GRATITUDE-FILLED THANKSGIVING

Napkins: handmade
Gratitude journals: handmade
Brass candleholders: vintage (thrift stores, antique malls, flea markets)
Assorted mid-century highball glasses: vintage (antique malls, thrift stores, eBay)
Assorted faux greenery: local craft stores
Terra-cotta wine holder: vintage (thrift store)
Table runner: handmade
Punchbowl and glasses: CB2

COLORFUL, MODERN CHRISTMAS DINNER

Bottle brush trees: vintage and local craft store
Wooden nutcrackers: local craft store
Small canvases: local craft store
Gauze napkins: handmade
Assorted barware: vintage (antique malls, thrift stores)

COZY WINTER BRUNCH

Colorful napkins: vintage (consignment store)
Neutral napkins: handmade
Brass/wood flatware: antique stores, estate sales, eBay
Side plates: vintage (thrift stores)
Juice glasses: vintage (thrift store)
Espresso mugs: vintage (thrift store)
Bud vases: Target
Small plates: wholesale purchase for hunt & gather
Letter cookie cutters: Amazon.com
Latte mugs: vintage (thrift stores)
Sugar bowl: Marshalls
Champagne flutes: Crate & Barrel

MEDIEVAL RUSTIC FEAST

Black flatware: Amazon.com
Assorted brass goblets and servingware: vintage (thrift stores, antique malls, ShopGoodwill.com)
Iron candelabras: vintage (thrift store and family pieces)
Large pitcher: ShopGoodwill.com

APRÈS SKI PARTY

Drink dispenser: Target
Bloody Mary glasses: wholesale purchase for hunt & gather
Beverage cart: Tuesday Morning
Pendleton table runner: fabric from Fancy Tiger Crafts
Lanterns: World Market

SPRINGTIME GARDEN FÊTE

Assorted glass bottles: vintage (antique malls)
Floral napkins: handmade (fabric from Fabric.com)
How to Draw Modern Florals and Florals by Hand books: Amazon.com

SHAREABLE TAKEOUT PARTY

White lanterns: Amazon.com
Assorted vintage lanterns: eBay
Takeout boxes: Amazon.com
Assorted chopsticks: vintage (antique malls)
Side plates: vintage (antique malls, thrift stores)
Old-fashioned glasses: World Market
Assorted vintage tea canisters: vintage (antique malls)
Napkins: handmade (vintage Indian block-print fabric from eBay)
Assorted tea towels: vintage (thrift stores)

FRIED-EVERYTHING PARTY

Baking tins: Target
Mason jars: vintage (estate sale)
Wooden serving bowls: Target, vintage
Plastic tumblers: King Soopers
Wooden coasters: local craft stores
Napkins: vintage (eBay)

LADIES WINE TASTING

Pink water glasses: IKEA
Napkins: World Market
Rattan screens: vintage (consignment shop, Craigslist)
Butcher paper roll: Amazon.com

PORTABLE PICNIC PARTY

Indigo fabric pieces: flea market
Picnic baskets: vintage (thrift stores)
Green water glasses: IKEA

TUSCAN TAVOLA

Napkins: handmade
Pitcher vase: T.J. Maxx
Blue water carafes: Miller Lane Mercantile
Italian lace tablecloth: eBay
Tube vases: thrift store
Cocktail coupe glasses: vintage (thrift store)

SUMMER BBQ BASH

Indigo cloths: flea market
Napkins: handmade (fabric from Fancy Tiger Crafts)
Coasters: vintage (Etsy)
Kombucha bottles: collected/recycled

BOHEMIAN BACKYARD BLOWOUT

Yurt: Amazon.com
Hand dishes: wholesale purchase for hunt & gather
Assorted votives: Anthropologie
Assorted woven fans: vintage (thrift stores)
Indian table runner: eBay

building your collection: a shopping list

Daily Collection

☐ Dinner Plate	8–12
☐ Salad Plate	8–12
☐ Flatware Set (five pieces)	8–12
☐ Water Glass	8–12
☐ Soup Bowl	8–12
☐ Pasta Bowl	4–6
☐ Fruit Bowl	4–6
☐ Mug	8–12
☐ Cups & Saucer	

Entertaining Collection

☐ Large Platter	2
☐ Medium Platter	4
☐ Large Bowls	2
☐ Soup Tureen	
☐ Gravy Boat	
☐ Cake Stands or Pedestal Platter	3–5
☐ Serving Utensil Set	3–4
☐ Wood Board	unlimited
☐ Condiment/Small Bowl	unlimited
☐ Basket	unlimited
☐ Small Plate	unlimited
☐ Steak Knives	8–12
☐ Large Pitcher	1
☐ Drink Dispenser	1
☐ Carafe	2
☐ Dinner Napkin Set	3–4 options
☐ Cocktail Napkin Set	2 options
☐ Tablecloth or Runner	unlimited

Bar Collection

☐ Wine Glasses	8–12
☐ Double Old Fashioned	4–8
☐ Highball	4–8
☐ Copper/Brass Mug	4
☐ Shot Glass	2
☐ Shaker or Mixing Glass	
☐ Cocktail Spoon	
☐ Bottle/Wine Opener	
☐ Measuring Shot Glass	
☐ Mixing Spoon	
☐ Beverage/Ice Bucket	

Decor Collection

☐ Taper Candleholder	10+
☐ Votive Candleholder	12+
☐ Assorted Vases	

acknowledgments

This book could not have been possible without the team at Blue Star Press guiding me through the process and believing in my idea. A big thanks also goes to my best friend, Alli Koch, for always inspiring me to grow, both in my business and myself.

Thank you to Colleen Cummings, Emily Bacon, and Margaret Shutze for sharing their homes with me for several photo shoots.

Thank you to all of my clients who have trusted me to help bring their love and authenticity to life for their wedding or event.

I could not operate my business, or have created this book without my family. To my mother-in-law, Bev, who flew into town on numerous occasions to watch my son as I prepared photoshoots, wrote snippets, or hauled around furniture. To my husband, Mark, who not only has endless belief and support for my work and my dreams, but also tolerates my many projects and collections. To my son, Alfeo, for going along with it all and always, always having the best time inventing new games and fun with all of my props and treasures. But most of all, to my parents, Karen and Guy, whose belief and love for me knows no end. They have always been there to push me and then lend a helping hand, whether figuratively or literally, talking through ideas, moving furniture, or hanging with their grandson. My family and friends' love and support continues to fuel and inspire me to new heights, and I will be forever grateful for my favorite people.

about the author

Photo by Abe Lopez-Brown, The Fort Co.

Amanda grew up in a family of party-goers and party-throwers and soon learned she was more of the latter. Her mother curated highly themed and highly detailed parties that now, thirty years later, friends and family still remember. Through college, Amanda used her party-planning skills for political parties and causes, and then through working with Greenpeace and other mission-oriented organizations. She later moved on to branding and content direction work for Fortune 500 companies, honing her eye for visual design paired with mission-centered messaging.

While planning her own wedding she launched hunt & gather design, offering event design and rentals with a modern bohemian twist. Today, after nearly 300 weddings and events, a husband, and a baby, she continues to curate events and editorial shoots and has grown her business into interior design, prop styling, and a lifestyle blog covering all aspects of modern bohemian lifestyles.

Her work can be seen in: *BRIDES* magazine, *Martha Stewart Weddings*, *Adweek*, *The New York Times*, *The Knot* magazine, *Green Wedding Shoes*, *Rocky Mountain Bride* magazine, *Wedding Chicks*, *Hello May* magazine, *Denver Style Magazine*, and more.

party planning tear sheet

Event: _____ Venue: _____

Date: _____ Expected No. of Guests: _____

Time: _____ Vibe/Takeaway Feelings: _____

_____

_____

MENU

Appetizers: _____

_____

_____

Main Dishes: _____

_____

_____

_____

Dessert: _____

_____

Wine: _____

_____

Cocktails: _____

_____

_____

EVENT DESIGN

What to Pull From Your Collection

Bar Setup

_____

_____

Table Setup

_____

_____

Food Service

_____

Setting the Scene

_____

_____

_____

TIMELINE FOR SET-UP

_____ : _____

_____

_____

_____ : _____

_____

_____

_____ : _____

_____

_____ : _____

_____

_____ : _____

_____

_____

_____

_____ : _____

_____

_____ : _____

_____

SHOPPING LIST

☐ _____
☐ _____
☐ _____
☐ _____
☐ _____
☐ _____
☐ _____
☐ _____
☐ _____
☐ _____
☐ _____
☐ _____
☐ _____

INVITE LIST

• _____
• _____
• _____
• _____
• _____
• _____
• _____
• _____
• _____
• _____